QUITE

BRILLIANT

A CELEBRATION

of

BRITISH

ENG

D1334106

HarperCollins Publishers
Westerhill Road
Bishopbriggs
Glasgow
G64 2QT

First Edition 2012

Reprint 10 9 8 7 6 5 4 3 2 1 0

© HarperCollins Publishers 2012

ISBN 978-0-00-748579-6

Collins® is a registered trademark
of HarperCollins Publishers
Limited

www.collinslanguage.com

A catalogue record for this book is
available from the British Library

Typeset by Davidson Publishing
Solutions, Glasgow

Printed in Great Britain by
Clays Ltd, St Ives plc

Acknowledgements
We would like to thank those
authors and publishers who kindly
gave permission for copyright
material to be used in the Collins
Corpus. We would also like to
thank Times Newspapers Ltd for
providing valuable data.

EDITORS
Gerry Breslin
Ian Brookes
Robbie Guillory
Andrew Holmes
Mike Munro

FOR THE PUBLISHER
Lucy Cooper
Elaine Higgleton
Kerry Ferguson
Susanne Reichert

CONTENTS

What Makes Britain Great?	vii
INSTITUTIONS AND CULTURE	1
The Fabric of a Nation	2
God Save the Queen!	4
Good Lord!	6
The Power House	8
Silence in Court!	10
Let Us Pray	12
Forward, March!	14
Money, Money, Money!	16
Degrees of Excellence	18
An Education in Itself	20
All Together Now!	22
Suits You!	24
All Aboard!	26
Home, Sweet Home!	28
Great Britons	30
It Takes All Sorts	34
Built to Last	36
Making Capital	38
Looking in the Mirror	40
The View from Abroad	42
ENTERTAINMENT	45
Britain at Play	46
At Your Leisure	48
All the Fun of the Fair	50
Let's Dance!	52
Beer and Skittles	54
Down at the Old Bull and Bush	56
Game for Anything	58
Good Sports!	60
The Place to Be	62

CONTENTS

Football Crazy   64
If You'll Pardon the Cliché   66
Flannelled Fools   68
Short, Square, and Silly   70
Quite Remarkable!   72

FOOD AND DRINK   75
The British Diet   76
The Local Speciality   78
Our Daily Bread   80
Who Ate All the Pies?   82
The Proof of the Pudding   84
A Piece of Cake!   86
Life is Sweet!   88
Taking the Biscuit   90
Say Cheese!   92
As British as Fish and Chips   94
Here for the Beer   96
Whisky Galore!   98

THE COUNTRYSIDE   101
The Great Outdoors   102
Down on the Farm   104
Tally-ho!   106
Our Feathered Friends   108
Hearts of Oak   110
A Floral Tribute   112
Under the Weather   114

WORK   117
Britain at Work   118
Just the Job   120
Thinking Outside the Box   122
Bank Statement   124

CONTENTS

OK Computer? 126

Everybody Out! 128

THE ENGLISH LANGUAGE 131

From Anglo-Saxon to Textspeak 132

Say It in Anglo-Saxon! 134

Waxing Biblical 136

Shakespeare Said It First 138

Anyone for Quidditch? 142

If You'll Pardon My French! 144

Britannia Rules the Waves! 146

All Present and Correct 148

Great Minds Think Alike 150

Why Not Get It Off Your Chest? 152

What the Heck? 156

Now There's a Funny Thing 158

You Are Awful ... But I Like You! 160

It's Good to Talk 164

Don't Call Me a Chav, Innit? 166

Dash It All! 168

A Little Bird Told Me 170

Out with the Old ... 172

... In with the New 176

A TOUR OF BRITAIN 181

A Disunited Kingdom? 182

Places with Strange-Sounding Names 184

Do You Know the Way to Silicon Fen? 186

Not from these Parts, Are You? 188

Maybe It's Because I'm a Londoner 190

Have a Butcher's at This! 192

There's Welsh, Boyo! 194

I'll Be in Scotland Afore Ye 196

In Sunshine or in Shadow 202

CONTENTS

A Life on the Open Road   206
Westward Ho!   208
Bostin' Brum   210
Of Mancs and Scousers   212
A Yorkshire Compliment   214
Howay, Man!   220

WHAT MAKES BRITAIN GREAT?

Britain is proud to call itself 'Great'. Indeed, having this word as part of our name does give the British a degree of self-confidence when we consider our country's place in the world. We may even sometimes imagine that the title 'Great' was conferred on us by a grateful community of nations as a reward for our general niceness and pluck.

In fact, 'Great Britain' is the name only of the largest island in the British Isles – the one that contains the mainland parts of England, Scotland, and Wales – although it can sometimes be taken to include the adjacent smaller islands such as the Isle of Wight, Anglesey, Orkney, and Shetland. The official name of the country in which we live is 'The United Kingdom of Great Britain and Northern Ireland'. The word 'Great' was originally applied to the island to distinguish it not (as you might think) from the smaller islands in the group but from another, smaller place called Britain, namely the area of Brittany in modern-day France.

Nevertheless, there is a widespread feeling among the British themselves that the name of 'Great Britain' is somehow an appropriate one. When we want to express our approval of something we regard as quintessentially British – anything from Marmite to the Mini – we are apt to say that it is 'one of the things that makes Britain great'. And it has to be said that, for a nation that prides itself on being humble and understated, there are a lot of things about which we like to congratulate ourselves: we created many of the world's most popular sports; we were also at the forefront of the Industrial Revolution; and our finest minds have made contributions to science and literature. Perhaps our greatest achievement, however, is the English language, which is now spoken by over 300 million people as a first language and by millions more as a second language. One in five people on the planet speaks English competently!

In this book we shall look at how the British way of life has contributed to the development of our language. Our journey will take us through seven different – although often intertwined – areas. We start by looking at some of the institutions that have shaped the country and at various aspects of British everyday life. Next we look at the different ways in which the British like to entertain themselves, whether through hobbies, games, or organized sport. Our third topic is food and drink, an area in which the British are much maligned and yet in which they have produced a number of distinctly palatable dishes. After this, we take a trip to the country and look at the names of the animals, birds, trees, and flowers that live and grow in these islands. Our fifth topic is the world of work, where recent developments have bought huge changes in both the way we live and the language we use. Our sixth topic is the English language itself: we trace its development from humble origins into its current state and explain some of its characteristic features. In our final section, we go on a tour of the different parts of the British Isles, looking in particular at how each region has its own slant on the English language.

In the course of our exploration we highlight hundreds of interesting words. The vocabulary of many British institutions is sometimes archaic or obscure and is often not known even to the British themselves, much less to those who visit these shores. The language of cricket, for example, is notoriously bizarre, while quite a few of us would have difficulty explaining exactly what a marchioness or an equerry is. Moreover, even when the words themselves are well understood, there are often intriguing histories behind them. In the pages that follow you will find out why pies are associated with a thieving bird, how a happy accident led to the creation of liquorice allsorts, why there are so many pubs called the Red Lion, and how the bowler hat was originally devised to protect gamekeepers on a Norfolk estate.

We do not pretend that this book offers a comprehensive treatment of its subject – there are many other elements besides the ones discussed here that contribute to that elusive quality of 'Britishness'. We hope, however, that the topics discussed in this book will help to give British people an insight into some things that have made their country what it is. Meanwhile, visitors from overseas should find explanations for some of the very puzzling things that the British say.

INSTITUTIONS *and* CULTURE

THE FABRIC
OF A NATION

Few things tell you more about a country than the way that it
chooses to organize itself. The way that we do things in Britain
has been shaped over centuries of history, involving invasions,
civil war, and the merging of the British nations into the United
Kingdom. The end result of this historical process is a set of
institutions that have some very distinctive features, and involve
some things with very odd names!

As we set out to learn what it is that makes Britain the country
that it is, we start off by examining how these institutions have
developed and how the language that they use often reflects their
old traditions. This is all very well for the people who are in the
know, but outsiders might need a bit of help if they are to
understand what is going on!

We start off at the top, looking at the role that the monarchy
and the nobility play in our society. These people may have the
big houses and the impressive titles, but they no longer hold any
real power in Britain, so we shall also look at the parliament that
governs the country and explain some of the terms and jargon
that it uses. After that we come to the great professions: the law,
the church, and the armed forces. We look at how the role of
these has changed over the course of the nation's history, and
explain some of the more colourful language that is associated
with them.

Another of the traditional professions is teaching, and
Britain's educational system has many intriguing facets. Both
our universities and our schools reflect strong historical divisions
between the privileged few and the masses. The older universities
of Oxford and Cambridge still preserve many of their old
traditions and use words that are unknown in a redbrick or
plate-glass institution; but the newer universities have their own
terminology too, and we should not exclude them from a survey

of how these bodies have shaped our language. Similarly, the traditions of the country's private schools are in marked contrast with the way that things are done in the state sector.

Of course, not all British people are involved in running the country and upholding its traditional institutions. We should also consider the contribution made by people going about their daily business. We shall look at a number of different areas that shed light on what it is to be British: what we do with ourselves, what we wear, how we travel from place to place, and where we live.

We also attempt to grasp some of the more abstract elements that make Britain what it is. We look at the historical figures we most revere, the places we hold dear, and the different types of people you might meet as you travel around the country. In looking at classic types of Briton we naturally invoke a few stereotypes, although there is usually some truth at the bottom of these caricatures!

We round off our look at British institutions and culture by taking two different views on the question of what it means to be British. We look at what the British themselves think, and then at how we are viewed by people in other countries. It seems that the elusive concept of 'Britishness' depends very much on where you come from. The British themselves like to assemble a list of national virtues, but those who live on other shores are only too keen to see our flaws!

GOD SAVE THE QUEEN!

The various nations of Britain have been ruled by a **monarchy** virtually from time immemorial, and it doesn't look like it is going away any time soon. Our current sovereign is Queen Elizabeth II, who celebrates her **diamond jubilee** in 2012 having spent sixty years on the throne. The 'II' can be a thorny issue in Scotland, which never had a Queen Elizabeth I, as her rule predated the Union of the Crowns. She is the second-longest reigning monarch that Britain has known, with only Queen Victoria having ruled for longer.

The British monarchy is a **constitutional** one, which means that though the Queen is our **head of state**, she agrees not to do any ruling or passing of laws and lets Parliament do the job instead. This system was put into practice in the seventeenth century when it was clear the idea that kings and queens ruled by 'divine right' spelled nothing but trouble. After the English Civil War the country managed without a monarch from 1649 to 1660, but then the restoration of Charles II with reduced powers proved a satisfactory compromise.

As our head of state the Queen has a number of duties, including appointing our prime ministers, attending the opening and dissolution of Parliament, and recognizing foreign countries, all of which come under what is known as the **royal prerogative**. This means that certain things cannot happen without the say-so of the reigning monarch, although there is an understanding that the government advises her majesty when such things should occur.

The **royal family** – consisting of the Queen and her close relatives – act rather like an extra corps of diplomats who can be deployed when a bit of royal clout might get things done, and as such they attend numerous functions each year. The Queen personally performs around two thousand duties a year, including everything from visiting a factory to hosting a garden party. Members of the royal family also lend their support to charities and other organizations that provide worthwhile voluntary service to the nation, often by becoming their patron or president to help them to raise funds and spread awareness. There are over three thousand organizations with a royal patron, and the Queen alone has more than six hundred to her name. No wonder she needs a bit of help from her **ladies-in-waiting** and **equerries** (formerly a person in charge of the stables, but now referring to any royal attendant).

A rather nice and relatively new touch is that the Queen will send you a card to congratulate you when you reach one hundred years of age, and also on your diamond wedding anniversary (reached after sixty years of marriage). These cards are personalized, but some recipients (you get a card every year over one hundred and five) have noted that the picture on the front doesn't change very often!

The **heir apparent** to the throne is known as the Prince (or Princess) of Wales. This practice began in 1301, when King Edward I proclaimed his son (whom he had ensured was born in Wales, in the mighty fortress of Caernarfon) to be the rightful holder of the title.

But the Queen is not sovereign of our small collection of islands alone. She is also the head of the **Commonwealth of Nations**, a group of fifty-two countries that used to be in the British Empire (plus Rwanda and Mozambique, which were never in the Empire but were allowed to join anyway). The members of the Commonwealth of Nations aim to cooperate together to improve progress in a number of different goals, such as furthering democracy and human rights, around the world. They also compete in a mini-Olympics, called the **Commonwealth Games**. The next games will take place in Glasgow in 2014.

GOOD LORD!

Until the Industrial Revolution the British **nobility** had pretty much run the country. These lucky members of a handful of privileged families sat in the House of Lords (which at this time was more powerful than the House of Commons), attended the court of whichever monarch was on the throne, and between them owned most of the land in Britain. Titles were hereditary, passed down from father to son over centuries (although in Scotland titles could go to women too). Since the nineteenth century, however, the powers held by this elite few have been diluted, and nowadays there is a limit on the number of **hereditary peers** who are allowed to sit in the Lords. The system that perpetuated the aristocracy cannot have survived for so long without a pretty sturdy hierarchy in place to keep those at the bottom stuck there. So here we list the order of precedence for the British nobility. Interestingly, it does not include the monarchy (kings, queens, princes, and princesses), although members of the royal family can also hold these titles.

Dukes and **duchesses** are the top dogs of the nobility. Nothing is nobbier than a duke. The estate of a duke is known as a **duchy**, but there is no fixed size that it should be. Perhaps the most famous of all British dukes was Arthur Wellesley, the 1st Duke of Wellington. The current Prince of Wales was given the title of Duke of Cornwall, while his son, Prince William was given the title of Duke of Cambridge.

Next in line come the **marquess** and **marchioness**. Henry IV reputedly said 'the name of Marquess is a strange name in this realm' and it must be said it is a very difficult word for us Brits to pronounce correctly. Not only that, but it has always had a very shaky relationship in Britain. The oldest **marquessate** (an estate that is like a duchy, but less important) is that of Winchester, and the holder of that title is called the 'Premier Marquess of England'.

After that are the **earl** and **countess**. Earls are in charge of
earldoms, and before the Norman Conquest were the powers
behind the throne(s) of Britain. William the Conqueror didn't
think much of the earls when he and his Norman lords took
charge, though, and their power was on a downward slope from
that point onwards. Harold Godwinson, Earl of Wessex, is
probably the best known earl in British history. He defeated
Harald Hardrada at the Battle of Stamford Bridge, but was
brought down with an arrow to the eye (or so the legend goes)
at the Battle of Hastings in 1066, having been King of England
for forty weeks and a day. He was the last Anglo-Saxon King of
England.

On the next rung of the nobility are perched the **viscount**
and **viscountess**. These can be either the holders of a **viscountcy**
or the heir of an earl or marquess, making it a very confusing title
indeed. Field Marshal Montgomery was awarded a viscountcy in
1945 after his sterling work commanding British, Commonwealth,
and Allied troops during the Second World War, particularly in
North Africa where he defeated the fearsome Afrika Corps.

The **baron** and **baroness** occupy the lowest branch of the
peerage tree, holding on to a **barony** and feverishly stamping on
the fingers of the landed gentry (although this title now exerts
less envy as there are no powers attached to it). In Scotland, the
rank of baron is outside of the peerage, and instead they have a
Lord (or **Lady**) **of Parliament** to hold this role.

THE POWER HOUSE

The Houses of Parliament is one of the most iconic buildings of Britain, standing on the banks of the River Thames, overshadowed by the slightly leaning clock tower, whose great bell, **Big Ben**, can be heard tolling the hours throughout the day and night. Not only is it a remarkable building, it also holds the two houses that govern Britain – the elected **House of Commons** and the unelected **House of Lords**. Outside the Palace you can find **Parliament Square**, which has often been a focal point for demonstrations against the government of the day.

The House of Commons is composed of 650 **members of parliament** (**MPs**), arranged on benches either side of a walkway. This arrangement dates from the time when parliament was dominated by just two political parties, known as the **Whigs** (Liberals) and **Tories** (Conservatives). Keeping them separate stopped any actual fighting, and also helped MPs remember which side they were on. In the House of Lords, a peer who claims to be member of no particular party is called a **crossbencher**, and can sit on either side of the hall.

Occasionally, an MP has been known to switch sides or **cross the floor** to join the other party. MPs who wish to leave the commons altogether apply for the nominal post of **Steward of the Chiltern Hundreds**, which historically was a diplomatic way of resigning your seat.

These days there are three large national parties (Conservative, Labour, and Liberal Democrat), as well as smaller parties and some parties local to Scotland, Wales and Northern Ireland. After a general election, the political party (or parties if a coalition is needed) with the majority of **seats** in the House of Commons is invited by the monarch to form a **government**, with the leader of that party usually becoming the **prime minister** (**PM**). Because Britain has a **constitutional monarchy** (the monarch is allowed to keep the crown and palaces as long as they don't actually try to run the place) this makes the prime minister the most powerful person in Britain. The PM is given a house at **Number Ten Downing Street** and a nice home in the country called **Chequers**.

The PM's first task on starting a government is to choose his or her **ministers** who can help share the power and make the job a bit easier. Those with responsibility for a department of government sit in the **cabinet** and are usually called **secretaries of state**, but the one in charge of the **Treasury** rejoices in the title of **Chancellor of the Exchequer**. This minister gets to live next door to the PM in Downing Street and say how much he or she is allowed to spend (if brave) or scrambles to find the money for all the PM's ideas (if weak). The parties that are not in power are known as the **opposition**, and it is their duty to make sure the PM and their party don't get away with anything too crazy.

The House of Commons is itself governed by the **Speaker of the Commons**, who is voted in by the MPs and is responsible for drawing up the schedule, counting the votes, and making sure the MPs are not too rude, always call each other 'the (right) honourable gentleman/lady', and never fight.

When voting on a particular subject, the MPs are summoned by the **division bell** to go to the **voting lobby** of their choice ('Aye' or 'No'), where they are counted. This isn't always a matter of individual conscience: a **three-line whip** means that all MPs are expected to vote in accordance with the party leadership regardless of their personal inclination.

SILENCE IN COURT!

British Law is split into three main parts: English, Scottish, and Northern Irish. This is simply because before the **acts of union** which created Great Britain, each individual country had already had plenty of time to make laws by themselves, and weren't all that keen on giving them up for one of the others statutes (a bit like the situation whereby each nation retains its own national football team).

As such, there are some large differences in how courts are run in each nation. For instance, a case under **Scots law** is worked on by **advocates** and **solicitors**, and you would not find a **lawyer** or **barrister** until you crossed the border into England.

The Scottish legal system is unique in that there are three possible verdicts (decisions, to you and me) that the accused can receive: **guilty**, **not guilty**, and **not proven**. The last two both mean that the accused is set free, but a 'not proven' verdict indicates that the acquittal is based on a lack of evidence rather than innocence ('we think he did it, but we can't prove it'). In English and Northern Irish law, most criminal cases take place in a **crown court**, where the judge and barristers wear the wigs and gowns that are often seen in television dramas. The judge is generally referred to as 'Your Honour' and everyone in the court has to stand up when the judge enters or leaves the court room.

The wigs (short for 'periwig') worn by judges and barristers are made of horsehair, and are generally white or grey, and are said to be rather itchy. They were, along with the gowns, once the fashion of the time, and slowly gained in popularity until they had become part and parcel of the drama of the courtroom.

To become a barrister (and hence gain your wig!) one must be **called to the bar** at one of the four **Inns of Court**, institutions that have existed for centuries as the home of English law. Every barrister, be they student or qualified, must belong to one of these Inns, even if their **chambers** (a group of barristers for hire) is not in London. Being called to the bar is the first step on the road to becoming a barrister, and simply means you have the right to cross the bar that separates the public from the court. If a barrister is very, very good at his or her job then they might be made **Queen's Counsel**, otherwise known as **taking silk**, meaning that not only do they get to wear silk robes, but also that they are recognized as being one of the best barristers in the profession.

Although sometimes the public are allowed to sit in on trials, it is illegal to make any sort of recording of what goes on in the courtroom except making notes on paper and the court **stenographer**, who writes a transcript. As such, there are never any photographs of court proceedings in Britain. However, **courtroom artists** are allowed to attend the court as a member of the public, and then draw what happened afterwards from memory! These sketches are usually done in charcoal or pastels, which can be used quickly on a bench outside the courtroom whilst the image is still fresh in the mind of the artist.

The top post as a judge is that of **Lord Chief Justice**, currently held by the perfectly named Lord Judge. This position is chosen by a panel made up of people connected to the legal profession, called the **Judicial Appointments Commission**. The Lord Chief Justice is responsible for choosing all the judges in England and Wales.

Some very strange cases have been brought before the British courts over the years. In 1991 the confectionary firm McVitie's was taken to court by Her Majesty's Customs and Excise to establish whether their popular Jaffa Cakes were cakes or biscuits. As value-added tax is levied on chocolate biscuits but not on cakes, this distinction would make a significant difference to the price of Jaffa Cakes in the shops. The court ruled that a Jaffa Cake is indeed a cake, and so was not subject to the tax.

LET US PRAY

In Britain, the church is not just a place where you can to take part in a religious service. The **Church of England** is an 'established' religion, which means that it is recognized by law as the official religious body of the county. Its highest authority – after God and Jesus, naturally – is not a bishop, but the Queen, who has a special title of **Defender of the Faith**. This position is perhaps something of an anomaly in the twenty-first century when Britain prides itself on being a multicultural society. Yet while British people are at liberty to follow other faiths – or no faith at all – the established Church has a special place in British culture.

The Church of England is divided into two provinces, one in the north (looked over by the **Archbishop of York**) and one in the south (run by the **Archbishop of Canterbury**). These two heads are known as **primates**, but that does not refer to the idea that we are all apes, but from the Latin meaning 'first', or head. The provinces are subdivided into **dioceses**, each overseen by a **bishop**, which are also subdivided until we reach the humble **parish priest**, who looks after a small collection of churches, or one well-attended one, perhaps with the help of a **curate**.

There are two main historical reasons for the existence of the Church. The first was the rise of Protestantism, which stated that religion should not require huge churches fitted out with gold and silver and ceremonies delivered in Latin. Protestants wanted to be able to control the way they talked to God, and did not want to be told what to do by the Pope, who is the head of the Roman Catholic faith. As well as this, the English king at that time was Henry VIII, who was desperate to divorce his first wife, Catherine of Aragon, and marry his mistress, Anne Boleyn, but the Pope would not hear of it. So Henry decided he could run a Church perfectly well without the Pope, passed an **Act of Supremacy**, and, hey presto, the Church of England was founded. Unfortunately for King Henry, the marriage to Anne Boleyn did not go as planned and he went on to marry six wives in total.

The Church of England has a unique say in how the country is run. In the House of Lords, the second House of our Parliament, there are twenty-six bishops known as the **Lords Spiritual**, who are supposed to bring a moral viewpoint to the laws being made. There are growing calls for these bishops to be split up so that more faiths can be represented, but nothing has been decided as yet.

The **Church of Scotland** is also an established Protestant Church, but it is run on rather more humble lines. Rather than the pomp and ceremony that still occurs in the Church of England, the Church of Scotland is run on **Presbyterian** lines. Presbyterianism is a more communal form of worship, where the Church is organized by a leadership made up of elected members (known as **elders**) and ministers, so that the authority is shared. The head of the Church is known as the **Moderator**, who is unpaid and elected each year, and all Church decisions are made at a yearly **General Assembly**. Although the Queen is not the official head of the religion on Earth, she is given a special place at each General Assembly. Similarly, although the Church is not officially represented in the Scottish Parliament, there are strong ties between the two, which makes sure that the laws passed receive an ample amount of moral scrutiny.

The Church of England looks after more than 16,000 churches, including 42 cathedrals and three world heritage sites. It is estimated that it would cost £185 million a year to maintain the properties in their current condition, but only about two-thirds of this amount is actually spent on renovation.

FORWARD, MARCH!

The armed forces of Britain are divided into members of the **Army**, **Navy**, and **Air Force**, including staff who do not see action on the battlefield. It isn't all about fighting wars and polishing boots, though looking smart on parade is always important! Here are some phrases associated with the forces:

❖ **Trooping the colour** is a parade that military regiments have performed for hundreds of years. These days it is ceremonial, but in the days when the regimental flag, or colour, was carried in to battle it was a matter of life or death that soldiers knew where their friends were.

❖ The **Edinburgh Tattoo** is an annual event that brings together many of the regimental bands of the Armed Forces for a grand spectacle of marching and sounds.

❖ The **Gurkahs** are members of the Royal Gurkah Rifles – soldiers recruited from Nepal to fight for Britain. They are famed as being some of the most dependable and bravest soldiers in the army, which they would have to be, as the selection process is one of the toughest in the world. Part of this is a test of strength and endurance where would-be recruits have to run uphill for forty minutes carrying a basket filled with seventy pounds of rock!

❖ **Beefeaters** (officially called **Yeoman Warders of the Tower of London**) are retired servicemen. They guard the historic **Crown Jewels** and help the tourists who visit the Tower. The **Ravenmaster** is tasked with looking after the Tower's raven population, as it is fabled that London will fall if the birds leave the tower.

❖ **Territorial soldiers** are ordinary civilians who sign up to receive military training and who are called up in times of war to fight alongside the regular army.

❖ The **redcoat** and **bearskin hat** are ceremonial dress of several British regiments. The red jacket came into being with the reorganization of the army by Oliver Cromwell in the seventeeth century, and was used right up to the late nineteenth century, when smokeless bullets meant that it was no longer so hard to be seen on the battlefield. You can still see soldiers in redcoats and bearskin hats guarding Buckingham Palace.

❖ The **NAAFI** – standing for 'Navy, Army, and Air Force Institutes' – has the task of keeping all military personnel fed, watered, and entertained. They run the **mess** areas, where solders eat, but also do the fighting when needs be.

❖ If you go walking around the area of Chelsea in London, you might see a number of old men and women wearing blue or red uniforms. These are the **Chelsea pensioners**, ex-servicemen living in a retirement home that keeps to strict military timings.

Some regiments have, in times of valour or stupidity, gained nicknames that reflect their deeds. One such is the 11th Hussars, a cavalry regiment who, during the Peninsular War of 1808–14, were taken by surprise by some French soldiers whilst they were foraging in an orchard and forced to fight on foot. Since that day they were known as the 'Cherry Pickers'. The regiment no longer exists, having been disbanded in the 1960s, but their name lives on with this rather embarrassing tale.

MONEY, MONEY, MONEY!

There are few objects that say so much about a country's image of itself as the coins that it issues. While other countries have their dollars, euros, and yen, Britain has the **pound** as its national currency. Bearing the image of the nation's sovereign, the pound is like a Union Flag in all our pockets. The heavy weight of it is easily distinguished from smaller coins (often dismissed as '**shrapnel**'). The very feel of a one-pound coin between thumb and forefinger is enough to make anyone feel rich.

As you would expect from something that has such a strong hold over our lives, the British have many different terms for the money in our pockets. We need **bread** in our wallets to buy the bread to put in our toasters, and as long as we have a lot of **lolly** we have no need to skimp on ice cream. Different amounts of money have their nicknames too, whether it is a **fiver** (£5), a **tenner** (£10), a **pony** (£25), or a **monkey** (£500).

In the past, coins were far more numerous than they are today. Our small collection of pounds and pence is known as 'new money', and has only been around since 1971.

'Old money' included such things as the **farthing** (worth a quarter of an old penny), **ha'penny** (half a penny), **thruppence** (three pennies), and **sixpence** (colloquially known as a **tanner**). The penny was much larger than the farthing, which led to an early bicycle with wheels of greatly different sizes being called a **penny farthing**.

Twelve pennies made a **shilling** (also known as a **bob**), two shillings made a **florin**, and five shillings made a **crown** (with a **half-crown** coin being worth two shillings and sixpence). Before 1971 the pound was worth twenty shillings, or two hundred and forty pennies. It was usually found as a paper banknote, but sometimes as a coin called a **sovereign**. Oh, and we must not forget the **guinea**, worth one pound and one shilling, which is still encountered today as the unit of prize money for some of our most notable horse races.

Coins are coined in the **Mint**, which is currently based in South Wales, but which for hundreds of years worked from the Tower of London. If you ran the Mint, you could, if you were clever, become very wealthy or 'minted', and the position of Master of the Mint was generally held for life. One of Britain's most famous scientists, Isaac Newton, was one such Master after his prior career engaged in sorting out the bad pennies from the good by investigating counterfeiting.

The penny has entered our language in a way that no other coin has managed. We 'spend a penny' when we go to the toilet, hear 'the penny drop' when someone understands us, say that expensive things 'cost a pretty penny', offer 'a penny for the thoughts' of others, try to 'turn an honest penny' from our work, and in return expect to 'get our pennyworth'.

Most pennies are struck from copper-plated steel these days, but an odd tradition going back hundreds of years says that on Maundy Thursday the reigning monarch hands out pouches of silver pennies, called **Maundy Money**, to pensioners. In the Middle Ages the monarch would also wash the feet of the poor, but for some strange reason this habit stopped at some point in the eighteenth century.

So, in for a penny, in for a pound, the coins that we collect, save, and spend are one of the cornerstones of British life.

DEGREES OF
EXCELLENCE

The United Kingdom is proud to be home to some of the oldest universities in the world – notably the elite quadrangles of Oxford and Cambridge (collectively known as **Oxbridge**). Other ancient universities include Saint Andrews, Glasgow, Edinburgh, and Aberdeen – all more than five hundred years old. At these ancient universities arts undergraduates work towards an MA (Master of Arts) degree, rather than the BA (Bachelor of Arts) awarded by most other places.

But there are lots of other universities in the UK. The term **redbrick university** refers to institutions founded in the Victorian Era, including Manchester, Leeds, and Bristol. They were originally regarded snootily by many traditionalists, but Britain's redbrick universities are proud to be some of the best research universities in the world, with all of them being members of the prestigious **Russell Group**.

There is a newer type of university to look down on now: the **plate-glass university**, so named because of the architectural style in which these were built. These were all built after the First World War, and it is here that the most radical of thinking and research often takes place. They include the University of York and the University of East Anglia. These are usually **campus universities**, meaning that rather than being in a city, they have their own surrounding grounds, with shops, pubs, and anything else students might need.

University students are awarded **degrees** in several different forms depending on how well the student has done. The best degree one can achieve is a **first-class** degree, and the worst (without failing) is a **third-class**, sometimes called a **gentleman's third**. If you have been very ill during your exams, but your tutors think you would have passed had you been able to take them, you might be awarded an **aegrotat** degree, which is a degree without a grade.

To be expelled from university is to be '**sent down**', or if the expellee is at Oxford or Cambridge then they may be '**rusticated**' (literally 'sent to the country') instead. To achieve this, it is generally agreed, requires an exceptional effort on the part of the student!

The rivalry between Oxford and Cambridge is nowhere better seen that at the annual **Boat Race** between the two universities on the River Thames. Several other sports are played between the universities in annual **varsity matches**, in which they go at each other hammer and tongs. The sportsmen and women who take part in these matches have all attained the **blue**, which means they are the best in their universities at that particular sport. Oxford and Cambridge are the only universities to award the blue, although they each choose a different shade – light blue for Cambridge and dark blue for Oxford.

Teaching at university comes in two forms: **lectures** and **tutorials**. Lectures involve students listening to their professors (also called lecturers) delivering a talk on a subject they know about, whereas tutorials are quite the opposite – students talking about things they have neglected to read up on. There is a perception that tutorials take place in cosy studies with a handful of students and the tutor pouring cups of tea, but sadly in most universities this is no longer the case.

Students sometimes refer to the different classes of degree by their slang names: a lower-second or 2:2 is called a **Desmond** (a pun on Desmond *Tutu*, the South African archbishop). Other names have been created by rhyming slang: a first is a **Geoff Hurst** (after the footballer); a 2:1 is a **Trevor Nunn** (after the theatre director); while a third-class degree is a **Douglas Hurd** (after the politician).

AN EDUCATION
IN ITSELF

The British education system can be confusing to outsiders. **Public schools** are anything but public, having long been the reserve of the British elite. Like other **private schools**, they charge fees for students to attend, although the rate varies from school to school. It is generally the case that these schools have a **uniform** that is worn at all times. A **boarding school** is a private school in which most students sleep on the school premises, either going home at the weekends, known as 'flexi-boarding', or only at holidays, which is known as 'full-boarding'. The students are separated into **houses**, which become a surrogate family whilst at school – all sporting or academic achievements are obtained for the glory of the house. Generally these houses are single-sex only, but there are some schools, such as Gordonstoun in Morayshire, that have mixed boarding houses.

One of the most famous public schools in Britain is Eton College. There the pupils still dress in a nineteenth-century uniform of pinstripe trousers and a black tailcoat. Although many other schools, both public and state, have uniforms, they are few so extraordinary that this. Eton is one of the last schools in Britain to still implement a form of **fagging**, where a young pupil is assigned to an older boy to carry out chores such as looking after his clothes and making sure he is up in the morning.

Tradition plays a major role in public schools, which see themselves as being guardians of Britain's institutions. For example, rather than the usual autumn and spring terms, private schools tend to call these by the more old-fashioned names of **Michaelmas term** and **Lent term**. School regimes are generally more traditional too, with the recital of **grace** at mealtimes and greater importance given to the pride of the school. It was thought that this sort of school, which takes a boy away from his family and 'makes a man of him', was necessary to create the so-called 'officer class' – the men who would take on the running of the country, its army, and its empire.

State schools are often more relaxed in the way they are run. The only cost for pupils in a state school is for a uniform (if necessary) and for their stationery. Everything else is provided by the state. The state education system is relatively uncomplicated until a pupil hits about eleven years old. After that there are several options.

Most pupils continue to a **secondary school**, which teaches them up to **GCSE** level at the age of sixteen, and can also include a **sixth form** (for **A-levels**, which are usually taken at the age of eighteen). These schools are run by the local councils, but there are a growing number of **academy schools**, which are under the direct control of central government and attract sponsors from the private sector. There are also a dwindling number of **grammar schools**, which are selective and are intended to provide a more focused learning environment to the cleverest students, irrespective of wealth. Scotland has a completely different school system altogether. On the whole it is an astonishingly complicated system, which is an education in itself.

Once you have reached sixteen, you are legally allowed to leave school without being called a **truant**, irrespective of whether you have attained any qualifications. Should you wish to continue to do A-levels (or **Advanced Highers** in Scotland), or to pursue a technical qualification in a subject such as joinery or construction, then you could go to a sixth-form college, of which there are both state and private examples.

ALL TOGETHER NOW!

Brits like nothing better than a bit of organization, be that meeting up to have a cup of tea or getting some chaps together to find the South Pole. We love plotting things out on charts, writing lists and crossing them out again, getting group A to point B, and then sitting them down with group C to have a chat about organizing something nice for group D who always come last but good on them for having a go. As such, we have a host of different clubs, societies, guilds, and committees, each doing their own bit of very British organizing. Here are a few:

❖ **Gentlemen's clubs** are quintessentially English, members-only clubs that are generally aimed at the upper classes or very rich. Most are in large houses in London, centred around the St James's district. These clubs offer a quiet place to read the paper, have a bite to eat, and maybe even take a short snooze. Being stopped from joining is called being **blackballed**, because a member could place a black ball in a bag as a veto. Notable clubs include The East India Club and Pratt's.

❖ **Working men's clubs** were started in the nineteenth century by trade unions to give their members a place to relax and be educated, and are still fulfilling this purpose today. Here you can get a cheap drink, have a game of snooker, and engage in a lively discussion. Membership is open to all, women included, despite the name.

❖ The **Freemasons** have a long and interesting past that is shrouded in legend upon legend. Originally a guild (or craftsman's society) for stonemasons, the order of Free and Accepted Masons now has members from every walk of life. You have to be asked to join, however, and there is said to be a secret handshake used to seek out other members. Masons meet in individual groups called **lodges**.

❖ The **Royal Society** is the oldest institution of its kind in Britain, and its members are some of the nation's finest minds. Started by Charles II, the society now acts as an advisor to the government on all things scientific. The society's motto is *Nullius in Verba*, meaning 'take nobody's word for it'.

❖ The **Scout Association** (and its sister organization the **Guides**) is a huge club, with over 28 million members worldwide, and yet it was started in England in 1907 by Robert Baden Powell, who wrote a book called *Scouting for Boys*. Children who are members of this organization enjoy adventurous activities, being taken into the countryside to camp and learn a bit of bushcraft. There are junior branches of the Scouts called **Cubs** and **Beavers**, while the junior Guides are called **Brownies** and **Rainbows**.

❖ The **Royal British Legion** is the biggest charity caring for current or former servicemen and women. Founded after the First World War, it funds research into post-traumatic stress disorder and provides legal help. It is best known for its poppy appeal, when artificial poppies are sold in the run-up to Remembrance Sunday, held every November to mark the end of the First World War.

❖ **Book clubs**, although organized on a much smaller scale than the rest, have seen a huge rise in popularity in recent years, and are evidence of the continuing desire for like-minded souls to get together. They involve everything we Brits like: a cup of tea, a book, and a chat.

SUITS YOU!

When it comes to fashion, there are two stereotypical views of the British man that cannot be avoided. The first is that of the suited Englishman, tightly rolled umbrella in hand and newspaper stuffed under one arm. The other is the rugged Scot, covered in tartan and probably playing the bagpipes and he stands on a hillside of heather. What says 'British fashion' more than these?

There are two streets in London that are known worldwide for the excellence of their tailoring: Savile Row and Jermyn Street. It is here that you will find the best examples of **bespoke** clothing. The **pinstripe suit** is known for being worn by bankers and business people, as is the **bowler hat**. The bowler hat was commissioned by a Lord Coke (pronounced 'cook'), the Earl of Leicester, who was annoyed that poachers were attacking the gamekeepers on his Norfolk estate. He wanted a hat they could wear that would look presentable but could also handle an almighty bash on the head. The bowler was the result, and it is rumoured that Lord Coke tested it by jumping on the prototype. Interestingly, in East London they are still referred to as Coke hats.

The **tie** is another article of clothing associated with the British suit. The most popular knot for a tie is the **Windsor knot**, which is variously said to have been invented by George V or Edward VIII, and thus could not be much more British if it tried. The shoes of our businessman would, in all probability, be **Oxford brogues**, though they could very well be a **Derby**, **monk**, or even a **ghillie**, if he happened to be going Scottish country dancing.

This takes us rather nicely to **Highland dress**, the other great British fashion statement. The famous **tartan kilt** was not really a part of Scottish identity until a visit to Scotland by king George IV in 1822 made them very popular. Since then, it has become a tradition for lowland Scots to wear Highland dress at special occasions. It has also become common to link tartans to **Scottish**

clans, and as such we now have a remarkable number of tartans available for almost every Scottish surname imaginable.

But the full Highland look would be nothing without the special extras that really give it an authentic look. A **sporran** is a must-have – a leather or fur pouch that hangs round the waist on a chain and is very handy as kilts have no pockets. Your sock is the place to keep your weapon, your **sgian-dubh**. This is a small, decorative, single-edged knife. It sticks out of the top of your sock – your right sock if you are right-handed, and the left if you are left-handed. The other accessory is the **Tam o' Shanter**, the traditional Scottish bonnet, named after a poem by the greatest of all Scottish poets, Robert Burns. Should you want to go the whole hog, you could add a **plaid** to your ensemble. This is a large piece of tartan that goes around the body and over the shoulder, and when worn correctly can look jolly impressive. Fear not, however, if the thought of the kilt gives you the jitters! You can always plump for a set of **trews**, which are tartan trousers – distinctly less draughty!

If you happened to decide on going tramping about the countryside whilst in Scotland, you would be wise to swap your kilt for a **tweed suit**, sometimes called '**thornproof**' due to its thickness and durability. The colour of tweed varies from area to area, depending on the colour of the landscape as tweed is intended to allow the wearer to blend into the background, so as not to frighten the wildlife away. **Harris tweed** is probably the best known of all tweeds and has been woven in the Outer Hebrides from local wool for at least two hundred years. Whilst out hiking it would also be wise to shrug off your brogues for a pair of **Wellington boots**, first worn by the Duke of Wellington and now popular amongst festival-goers across the world.

ALL ABOARD!

There are probably more ways to get around Britain than there are places you would like to visit. You name it, and we probably have it (but not the bullet train, alas). In fact, Britain has long been a pioneer in forms of transport. The ground beneath our feet has rumbled to the rhythm of the first tube system, passenger railway, bicycle, and many more forms of locomotion. We like to be able to go places, and we like to get to those places on time. But all this invention and experimentation has led to some rather specialized terms. Here are a few to help you find your feet.

❖ The **Routemaster** bus, along with the black cab and the Underground, is one of the hallmarks of transport around London. This iconic bright red, double-decker bus is returning to London streets as of 2012 in a new, updated format for the city's Olympic Games.

❖ The British canal system is a beautiful thing, and one can travel the length of England with ease. A **narrowboat** is a vessel peculiar to England, because some of our canal systems were built narrower than usual in the eighteenth century to cut costs. Narrowboats are often colourfully painted, and although they were once used for the transportation of goods, they are now more often used as homes.

❖ There are a number of underground railways in Britain, the most notable being the London Underground (often called the **Tube**), the Tyne and Wear **Metro** in Newcastle, and the Subway in Glasgow (occasionally called the '**Clockwork Orange**' because of its colour and its circular route). Although sometimes seen by outsiders as being an uncomfortable way to travel, these systems are embraced proudly by each city's inhabitants as being a symbol of their status and a link to their industrial and economic past.

- ❖ At the beginning and end of the school day, Britain's roads are filled with **Chelsea tractors** – large 'people carriers' used by parents who clog up the network on the **school run**. This informal name comes from the fact that a type of vehicle that was previously seen only on farms suddenly began to appear on the narrow streets of London, generally in the more wealthy areas.

- ❖ If you see a white square with a red L printed on it attached to the front or back of a car, drive with caution! These **L-plates** are signs indicating that the person behind the wheel is still learning to drive. Seeing these plates on the car in front might be a cause for concern, but please remember that they will always be more terrified of you than you are of them.

- ❖ If you see a collection of white lines across the road in front of you, watch out for pedestrians crossing. There are a variety of different pedestrian crossings in Britain, conventionally named after different animals, but they always have the black and white lines to warn you. For **pelican crossings** (for pedestrians only), **toucan crossings** (pedestrians and cyclists) and **Pegasus crossings** (pedestrians, cyclists, and horse riders), you will also have the benefit of traffic lights to warn you when to stop. For **zebra crossings**, on the other hand, it is the pedestrian who has the right of way! You should be alerted to a zebra crossing by the presence of **Belisha beacons** – two amber coloured globes atop black and white striped poles. The Belisha beacon takes its name from Leslie Hore-Belisha who was a Minister of Transport during the Thirties.

HOME, SWEET HOME!

An Englishman's home is his castle, as the saying goes, and it is true that our houses are very close to our hearts, even though very few of us actually live in castles! In fact very few Britons would relish living a draughty old building that is a nightmare to heat, ruinously expensive to run, and contains more rooms than make sense. Instead, many of us dream of one day having a little house in the country with flowers around the door, where we might tend a garden and grow our own vegetables.

At one time there were almost as many types of dwelling in the British Isles as there were types of people, and many buildings retain names that hint at the professions that were once carried out in them. In rural villages you are likely to find a **smithy** or **forge** that was owned by a blacksmith in the past, or maybe a **mill**, **farmhouse**, **schoolhouse**, or **bakery**. The village priest or minister in Scotland lives in a **manse**, which is generally the biggest house in the village and sits near the church. In England such a house is more likely to be called a **vicarage**. Historically, many Scots lived in **crofts**, where (in theory) a family could grow its own food and be completely self-sufficient. These would often be rented from the laird, the owner of an estate in the area, but now they are regularly bought outright.

A house is usually the most expensive purchase made in a person's lifetime, but the British place a premium on owning their own homes, and we are all desperate to get on the **property ladder**. Generally, to buy a house you apply for a **mortgage** from the bank, and hope that the enormous sum – usually around three times your annual income – can be paid back eventually. You then have to go **house hunting**, but luckily this doesn't require any dangerous equipment. Once you have found a house, you put an offer in for it, trying to get a lower price than the seller is asking for. If you are very ruthless, then you could try to **gazunder** the seller by lowering your offer at the last minute, but make sure that you get that acceptance in writing or it might be **gazumped**!

This is where the seller agrees to your offer verbally, but then uses that verbal agreement to solicit a higher offer from someone else.

When looking at property, it is of course very important to know what sort of house you are looking for. At the cheaper end of the market are the **back-to-back** (which is attached to other properties on three sides) and **terraced** house (a small house that is part of a row of identical properties). From there you might graduate to a **semi** (a house connected only to one other) or even a **detached** house (one that stands alone, often with a garden between it and the next building). Right at the top of the property ladder is the **stately home**, a huge building in the country, with acres of garden and more baths than most people have rooms. However, buyers should beware that a **country estate** is very different from an **inner-city estate**: one will generally contain lots of fields and woods and maybe a trout pond or two, whereas the other is a place where lots of people are packed in to a very small area.

> The Queen is one of the biggest landowners in the country. In addition to the 6400 hectares of land that she owns, she also owns roughly 55% of British beaches!

GREAT BRITONS

Every nation has its heroes – people whose faces appear on its banknotes and whose statues grace the public spaces in its cities – and Britain has certainly produced its fair share over the last 2000 years. Here we salute some of the iconic figures who have saved or inspired the nation and are held up as examples of the great British virtues.

Boudicca (also known as **Boadicea**; died 62AD) was the queen of the Iceni tribe in East Anglia, who became a figurehead for native resistance to the occupation of Britain by the Romans. After some initial successes her rebellion was crushed and she poisoned herself.

King Arthur is a semi-legendary figure thought to have died in battle in the sixth century and have been buried at Glastonbury in Somerset. The historical Arthur has become mythologized as a great leader who unified the British tribes and set up a dazzling court at Camelot where his knights sat around a round table and ventured out on quests to find the Holy Grail – the bowl used by Jesus at the Last Supper. Many writers have been inspired by the legend of Arthur, the 'once and future king' who, it is said, will return to help his country at the time of its greatest need.

Alfred the Great (849–99) is the only British king to have earned the nickname 'the Great', although he was actually only the king of Wessex in the west of England. He repelled invasions by the Vikings and was a great patron of literacy, although the most famous story associated with him relates how he was asked by a peasant woman to sit by the fire and watch some cakes and was then scolded when he absent-mindedly let them burn. We do like to focus on our heroes' flaws, don't we?

Hereward the Wake (who died around 1072) led the Saxon opposition to the conquering Normans after the Battle of Hastings. He is one of many historical figures whose status as a rebel and an underdog have appealed to the British, and his deeds were later romanticized in fiction.

Richard the Lionheart (1157–99) must have one of the best nicknames of any British ruler. He was noted as a leader during the Crusades, when Europeans tried to recapture Jerusalem from Muslim control. Unfortunately the facts of Richard's life don't quite live up to the PR: he didn't speak English and spent only a few months of his reign in his kingdom, leaving the people to be fleeced by his brother, bad King John.

Robin Hood is another semi-legendary figure, said to have lived during the reign of Richard the Lionheart. According to the legend he lived as an outlaw in Sherwood Forest with his band of 'merry men' who robbed from the rich and gave to the poor. In spite of his associations with the city of Nottingham he was probably active – if he existed at all – in south Yorkshire.

Sir **William Wallace** (c.1272–1305) is a national hero in Scotland, noted for his defeat of the English army at Stirling Bridge in 1297. He is commemorated by the huge Wallace Monument just outside the city of Stirling. He was relatively unknown outside Scotland before the 1995 film *Braveheart* brought his story to a worldwide audience.

Robert the Bruce (1274–1329) led the Scots to their greatest victory over the English at the battle of Bannockburn in 1314. His spectacular military successes are said to have been inspired by watching a spider while hiding after a military defeat. The spider made several unsuccessful attempts to construct its web before it eventually succeeded, thus demonstrating the virtues of persistence to the despairing king.

Owain Glyndŵr (c.1350–c.1416) occupies a similar role in the hearts of Welsh people as William Wallace does for the Scots. He led a prolonged guerrilla campaign for Welsh independence from the English and was the last Welshman to be proclaimed Prince of Wales.

Henry V (1387–1422) was the victor of the battle of Agincourt in 1415, when a small English army routed a much larger French force. He is immortalized in the plays of Shakespeare as a rakish youth who accepts his destiny and becomes a great warrior king.

Elizabeth I (1533–1603) is noted for her long reign which coincided with a flowering of culture (notably in the works of Spenser, Marlowe, and Shakespeare), trade, and English maritime supremacy.

Sir **Francis Drake** (c.1540–c.1596) was the first Englishman to sail around the world, but is best known for defending England against a Spanish invasion in 1588. The casual nonchalance with which he took his time over finishing a game of bowls before going out to defeat the Spanish armada fostered a belief in the amateur spirit that did not bode well for British sporting success in later generations.

Oliver Cromwell (1599–1658) led Britain during its only period without a monarch, having defeated the Royalist party in the English Civil War. Cromwell's Puritans are characterized as being 'right but repulsive' in comparison with the Royalists, who were 'wrong but romantic'. He is perhaps not the most likeable of historical figures, but his determined pursuit of his moral convictions earns him a grudging respect.

Sir **Isaac Newton** (1642–1727) is probably Britain's greatest scientist. He is supposed to have begun work on establishing the laws of gravity after watching an apple fall from a tree in his garden. His image formerly appeared on British one-pound notes.

Viscount **Horatio Nelson** (1758–1805) was Britain's greatest naval commander. He was killed at the battle of Trafalgar after masterminding the defeat of the French and Spanish fleets. He is commemorated by Nelson's Column in London's Trafalgar Square.

Arthur Wellesley, the first **Duke of Wellington** (1769–1852), is famous for giving Napoleon a good biffing at the battle of Waterloo in 1815. Hundreds of British pubs are named after him, as well as a pair of boots. He was actually born in Ireland, which at the time was part of the United Kingdom.

Florence Nightingale (1820–1910) became famous for her work as a nurse during the Crimean War, when she was known as 'the Lady with the Lamp'. She helped to raise the status of the nursing profession and founded a training school for nurses in London.

Captain **Robert Falcon Scott** (1868–1912), known as 'Scott of the Antarctic', commanded two Antarctic expeditions and reached the South Pole in January 1912, only to find that the Norwegian Roald Amundsen had got there first. He and the rest of his party died on the return journey, but his heroic failure fits him squarely in the mould of the classic British hero.

Sir **Winston Churchill** (1874–1965) is noted for his leadership of Britain during the Second World War, when his speeches and radio broadcasts helped to inspire the nation. He served as a member of parliament for nearly 64 years and was the first British politician to be given a state funeral. In a BBC poll in 2002 he was voted as the greatest Briton of all time.

Diana, Princess of Wales (1961–97) is probably the most iconic British figure of recent times. Formerly Lady Diana Spencer, her marriage to Prince Charles in 1981 made her famous around the world as she brought new glamour to the royal family. The marriage ended in divorce in 1996, and her death in a road accident the following year brought unprecedented scenes of public grief.

IT TAKES ALL SORTS

Anyone who has travelled around Britain will realize that these islands contain many different types of people. In some cases these types have changed British politics or made huge impacts on our cultural heritage. Here is a selection of stereotypical creatures you might encounter.

- ❖ **Essex man** was the name given to the sort of working-class Conservative voter who helped to keep Margaret Thatcher as Prime Minister in the 1980s. A decade later **Mondeo man** (named after the car he would be expected to drive) was of a similar demographic but the target of Tony Blair's Labour Party in the 1997 election campaign.

- ❖ Unlike the Essex man, **Essex girl** has not had a big impact on British politics, but could be the reason behind a lot of our current pop and television culture. Essex girl wants to be posh, but can only do it on the cheap. Expect fake tan, extravagantly painted nails, and a keen interest in celebrity.

- ❖ **White van man** is not restricted to a particular county but can be seen across Britain. As you may have guessed, he is the owner of a white van. Notorious for terrible driving, bouts of road rage, and a lack of consideration for anyone else, coming up against such a figure drives terror into the hearts of any motorist.

- ❖ **City slickers** – also known in some parts of the country as a '**grockles**' – are people for whom the countryside is not just another country, but another universe. Sometimes found lost in country lanes complaining about the mud on their tyres, city slickers take to the unkempt green places like a fish out of water, and should be dissuaded from ever leaving their concrete jungles.

❖ Almost the exact opposite of the city slicker, the **country bumpkin** is renowned for never having visited a city, and for tracing his lineage through generations of farm labourers, often from the same village. Seen as being in steep decline, owing to the lack of work, beware their thick regional accents if asking for directions!

❖ The **Sloane Ranger** is named after the affluent area around Sloane Square in London. **Sloanies**, as they are sometimes known, are generally dressed in the most expensive of clothes, have been educated at a private school, and share a most expensive lifestyle. They can also be known as Hooray Henrys, Yahs, and Ruperts.

❖ One of the abiding, albeit outdated, British stereotypes is that of the **gentleman's gentleman**, a butler-valet with an encyclopedic knowledge and a good nose for classic fashion. As a butler he will bring you breakfast in bed, keep your house in fine order, tell people you want to avoid that you are out, and usher in those you like. As a valet he will care for your clothes, pack your suitcases when you go on holiday, and will even run you a bath in the morning. The epitome of this type is Jeeves, the astute butler created by the novelist PG Wodehouse.

❖ The Welsh are renowned for two things in particular: their skill at rugby and their ability to produce wonderful singers. Hearing a **Welsh male-voice choir** is a very spiritual experience, as is listening to the crowd belt out 'Land of my Fathers' at the start of a Six Nations rugby match.

BUILT TO LAST

We are blessed in Britain with some of the finest architecture on the planet. From ancient druidic sites to the gleaming glass of the Gherkin, we have it all, and some of them offer great views! Here are a few British buildings that we think are especially iconic.

- ❖ **Stonehenge** is a circle of standing stones, some of them dragged for 150 miles from Wales to be erected for a purpose no one has yet managed to fathom. It is a popular destination for watching the winter and summer solstices, especially amongst the druid community that still remains active in Britain, although nowadays they have to practise their faith from behind the fence that protects it.

- ❖ **Westminster Abbey** is not only the place where coronations have taken place since 1066, but has also hosted royal weddings and quite a number of funerals too. Many monarchs have been laid to rest in the Abbey, as well as some of our brightest minds, including Geoffrey Chaucer, Isaac Newton, and Neville Chamberlain. The **Poets' Corner** is a notable burial site, as it contains many of Britain's greatest writers and artists.

- ❖ When it was built, the **Forth Bridge** was so long that as soon as they finished painting it, it was time to start again at the beginning. The expression 'painting the Forth Bridge' is therefore used to describe a never-ending task (although because of the recent advances in chemistry the current paint job will actually last for twenty-five years before it needs to be redone). This beautiful cantilever bridge connects Edinburgh with the kingdom of Fife, and is an emblem of the advances that Britain achieved in engineering and manufacturing in the nineteenth century.

❖ **Hadrian's Wall** is not quite the furthest north the Roman Empire managed to get in Britain (the **Antonine Wall** has that honour) but is a magnificent statement all the same. Built on the instructions of Emperor Hadrian, it has come to be regarded as a symbolic boundary between England and Scotland. It stretches the full width of the country from the Solway Firth in the west to the aptly named Wallsend in the east, and is still very visible today. As a statement of the end of a great civilization it is magnificent; as a route for walking it is breathtaking.

❖ Just as Hadrian's Wall symbolizes the border between Scotland and England, **Offa's Dyke** divides England from Wales. It is a massive ditch that was carved from the earth in the eighth century. Little is known of Offa, except that he ruled the Mercian Kingdom (now the English Midlands) and had this dyke built as fortification against the kingdom of Powys (Wales).

❖ If you drive north up the A1(M) you can see the **Angel of the North** rising out of the countryside as you pass Gateshead. One of the greatest pieces of modern sculpture in Britain, it was designed by the sculptor Anthony Gormley as a symbol of the industrial power of the north, and was built in Hartlepool out of 200 tons of steel.

❖ A new addition to the London skyline, the **Gherkin** is, well, shaped rather like a gherkin, although this one is 180 metres tall, covered in plate glass, and has a bar at the top. Whether they sell gherkins there is unknown.

MAKING CAPITAL

The great eighteenth-century writer Samuel Johnson said that 'when a man is tired of London, he is tired of life'. Whether this is the case or not is worth some debate, but it cannot be denied that there is something mesmerizing about the city of **London**. With a population larger than that of Scotland, London is the magnetic heart of Britain, dragging towards it knowledge, people, and wealth. It was not lightly that Benjamin Disraeli, one of Britain's greatest Prime Ministers, called it 'a nation, not a city'.

Being the capital city of Britain – and for 300 years of the British Empire – London has amassed a large number of magnificent buildings, palaces, and statues, and it is undeniable that no other city in Britain has so much to look at. From the Palace of Westminster to Westminster Abbey, Nelson's Column to Piccadilly Circus, it is a visual feast for any traveller from abroad or country bumpkin arriving to seek his fortune. Most of the London we see today was built after 1666, when the **Great Fire of London** swept through the city and destroyed thousands of houses. Though a terrible disaster, it did have some good points. Firstly, it put an end to the plague that had been ravaging the city, and secondly had it not burned down, among others, the old wooden St Paul's Cathedral, we would not have the magnificent new version by Christopher Wren to gaze at to this day.

In the previous couple of centuries, when we burned coal like it was going out of fashion and had not the faintest notion about global warming, London was known to get terrible bouts of smog, or 'pea-soupers' as they were known. In 1802 William Wordsworth wrote a famous poem about standing on Westminster Bridge one early morning and being amazed at finding the city smoke-free and beautiful. Although the air is now generally free of smog, and we can see the wonders of the city at almost any hour of the day or night, London is still referred to as '**the Big Smoke**' today.

London is a fascinating place to visit and explore. If the being there is more important to you than the getting there then it might be worth your while going in a black cab, because cabbies are known to have **the knowledge**, an encyclopedic understanding of all the narrow streets and one-way systems across all the London boroughs. There are thirty-two boroughs in London, each of which is run by its own council. Most boroughs are referred to as the 'London borough of ...', except for Westminster, which has the status of a city, and four **Royal boroughs**: Kensington, Kingston upon Thames, Chelsea, and Greenwich. The difference between the two sorts of borough is almost non-existent, as the naming just means that a monarch has at some point offered the borough patronage. For instance, Kensington became a royal borough because Queen Victoria was born in Kensington Palace, whereas Kingston upon Thames is royal because, in the tenth century, king Athelstan was crowned there.

One of the most confusing things about London for outsiders is that there is a difference between London (the city) and **the City of London**, which is a square mile of land towards the middle of London and is a city all of its own, with a separate police force, mayor, and by-laws. This is where most of the country's financial offices are based, and so when you hear people referring to 'The City' in a business sense they are referring to the City of London.

> Every year the livery societies of the City of London elect a Lord Mayor. The office dates back to 1189, when Henry Fitz-Ailwin was the first incumbent, but probably the most famous person to hold the post was Dick Whittington, whose story is the basis of a popular pantomime. He served four terms in 1397, 1398, 1406, and 1419. Only one woman has ever served as Lord Mayor – Dame Mary Donaldson, in 1983.

LOOKING IN
THE MIRROR

Britain is made up of four nations, and an innumerable number of distinct cultural groups, each with very different views of themselves and of each other. Whether you are English, Northern Irish, Welsh, or Scottish, we know who we are and what we think of each other. As such, the idea of a uniform '**Britishness**' is a tricky one to define, and is only likely to fan the flames of the squabbles between our nations.

Perhaps the most important tie that binds us together is that of the building of the British Empire, and our mixture of pride and embarrassment in it, and also of being an island nation with a famous seafaring past. When James Thomson wrote the words 'Rule, Britannia, rule the waves; Britons never will be slaves' our mastery of the oceans was near complete, and continued for a further two hundred years. We see ourselves as intrepid explorers, always willing to do what is right for 'Queen and Country', keeping a **stiff upper lip** and, perhaps most of all, determined to play within the rules (as long as we see those who we are playing against as equal). We are unbendable in our regard for traditions and the monarchy – as Sir Hugh Casson said, 'The British love permanence more than they love beauty.' Although this judgment is perhaps a little on the harsh side, we are usually happiest when things stay the same, and anyone seeking change has a tough time of it.

There is a figure called **John Bull**, who is the national personification of Britain (as is **Britannia**, although she represents more the spirit of Britain, and John Bull more the idea of Britishness). He is usually drawn to look like a stout, middle-aged man, stubborn, often dressed for living in the country, and often with a **Union Jack** waistcoat. It would be hard to find a better representation of the British mindset!

The Scottish national identity is very strong, and Scots see themselves as a people of great potential. And quite rightly too, as many of Britain's greatest inventions, from the refrigerator to the telephone, have come from the rugged north of Britain. Scots have a ruthless attitude to business and design – as JM Barrie once noted, 'There are few more impressive sights in the world than a Scotsman on the make.' A large part of the Scottish identity stems from the belief that Scotland is too often playing second fiddle in the running of Britain, an ideal that the Scottish actor Sean Connery (who played the quintessential Englishman, James Bond) holds dear to, having said that 'Scotland should be nothing less than equal with all the other nations of the world'.

England's role as the senior partner in the union has meant that many of the attributes that go to make someone 'British' are seen as the same as those that make them 'English'. The English see themselves as a moral compass, a leading light on the world stage and not afraid to stand up to larger nations. They pride themselves on their respectability and their quiet manner of keeping calm and carrying on. James Agate noted that 'the English instinctively admire any man who has no talent and is modest about it'. And it is true that above all being English is about not boasting but instead being a team player. Without order there could be no England, no quiet respectability. As the Anglo-Hungarian author George Mikes once remarked, 'An Englishman, even if he is alone, forms an orderly queue of one.'

THE VIEW FROM ABROAD

It has to be said that the view of Britain from abroad is not a very appealing one. The British tourist has a reputation of being sunburnt, unwilling to try anything foreign (especially another language), being too loud, and of constantly complaining that a German has taken the last sun lounger. The fact of the matter is, if you have spent the last thousand years or so fighting your neighbours, bossing them about, and paying pirates to steal their gold, you are going to build a pretty awful reputation, no matter how well you might have behaved in the last sixty years.

In France, Brits are known as '**les rosbifs**' – the roast beefs, in a scathing attack on British cuisine. Brits happen to like a roast and two veg on a Sunday, but on the continent it is viewed as a pretty awful way to treat food. Napoleon Bonaparte famously said that the British are 'a nation of shopkeepers' – suggesting that they were unfit to fight him. Instead the opposite was true, and our wealthy 'shopkeepers' were able to fund a very powerful army to set against him. During World War One '**Tommy**' became the accepted name used for all British soldiers by the French and Commonwealth nations, due to the name '**Tommy Atkins**' which was used on all sample forms and pay books in the British Army, and was often used by German soldiers when shouting across trenches.

In South Africa it is the British susceptibility to the sun that the Afrikaners pick on, calling Brits '**rooineks**' – red necks. And the Germans, referring to the reputation of loutish behaviour abroad, call Brits '**inselaffen**' – island monkeys! Interestingly, in Chile British people are often called Scottish, owing to the large number of Scots who migrated to South America from the eighteenth century onwards.

In America they refer to the British as **limeys**, which at first seems a very odd thing to call anyone. It all comes down to period in the eighteenth century when the British Navy lost more men to scurvy (a severe lack of vitamin C that causes jaundice and gum disease) than to fighting, and as such was desperate to find an antidote to this drain on its resources. Once it was discovered that scurvy was caused by a deficiency in vitamin C, the Navy started to issue a lime ration to all its men, limes being in plentiful supply on the Caribbean islands under British rule!

The weather has only compounded the British reputation abroad. One Australian is said to have opined that 'there were only three things against living in Britain: the place, the climate, and the people.' Pretty damning all round really, but then the Australian perception of us is not improved by the **whingeing Pom**, a British tourist or immigrant who moans about everything Australia has to offer. Our antipodean cousins also think Brits could do a lot to improve their personal hygiene, using the expression '**as dry as a Pommy's towel**' and calling deodorant a '**Pommy's shower**'.

At the very best, Britain is a country of oddity. The American philosopher George Santayana remarked that 'England is the paradise of individuality, eccentricity, heresy, anomalies, hobbies, and humours.' He is quite right, of course. One of the things that sped Britain's progress in the Industrial Revolution was the fact that the inhabitants of the islands were unafraid to take to their garden sheds to build some mad invention they had dreamt up the night before. Eccentricity is loved and cherished, and those eccentrics often become our national treasures.

ENTERTAINMENT

BRITAIN AT PLAY

The British have always made the most of their spare time. Even during the distant period of our history when most of the people worked on the land, shepherds invented games that involved throwing balls through wicket gates, while the agricultural and religious feasts were passed in communal dancing or in competitions that pitted neighbouring villages against each other. Nowadays most of us are fortunate in having plentiful leisure time and there is no shortage of ways in which to use it. This section of the book sheds some light on the sort of things that British people like to do to entertain themselves, and spotlights the words that have entered the English language as a result.

The traditional calendar included festivals and fairs in which the whole community got together. These have largely fallen into abeyance, although some areas still maintain proud local traditions. Yet most communities still observe a special local holiday during the course of the year. Even if the activities that take place have changed, the old names often survive.

One of the chief forms of entertainment practised at the old festivals was dancing, and we shall look at the traditions associated with that activity, from its pagan roots to its modern reinvention as Britain's favourite television viewing experience. After all that jumping around you might need to have a drink, and where better to quench your thirst than the village pub? We shall pop into the snug for a swift half and play some pub games, pausing on the way out to take note of some of the stories behind traditional pub names.

The mention of games brings us to the subject of organized sport. Britain is proud to think of itself as the cradle of many sports. The country's position as a great organizer and codifier of games can be traced to its imperial past. The Duke of Wellington is supposed to have said the Battle of Waterloo was won 'on the playing fields of Eton', alluding to the idea that team sports – as taught in Britain's public schools – helped to foster the traits of comradeship, determination, and respect that provided the nation's youth with an ideal military training.

Sport is no longer regarded as training for building an empire, but it is still encouraged as a healthy and character-building activity, although many prefer to watch from the comfort of their armchairs. We will look at the way that sport has become a part of the British establishment, and how certain places in the country have become synonymous with sports that are played there. We then take a more in-depth look at the nation's two favourite sports: football is regarded as the nation's winter game (although fans of rugby might dispute that!), while cricket is the game that occupies us in the summer months. We shall look at some of the use (and misuse) of language for which football is held responsible before getting to grips with the peculiar nomenclature that is attached to the game of cricket. But, if after reading this you still can't tell a third man from a square leg, then don't worry – many Brits don't have a clue about this either!

The variety of entertainments to be found within the British Isles is hugely impressive, and this book can only touch on a fraction of the things that people do to have fun. If the hobbies and games described here don't appeal to you, there's sure to be something else that will – but at least you'll now understand some of the obscure terminology of the games we play!

AT YOUR LEISURE

The British have 'an addiction to hobbies and spare-time occupations'. So said George Orwell in the 1940s, but the same can still be said. Some of the hobbies he spoke about as 'communal [but] not official' are thriving to this day. Pigeon fancying and allotment tending are two that have provided quiet enjoyment, and fierce competition, to many people's spare time.

Pigeon fancying is a sport in which a 'fancier' breeds and trains homing pigeons. The birds are taken to a starting point where they are 'liberated' and then fly back to a loft which is in or attached to their owner's house. The winner is the bird covering the journey at the highest average speed. It emerged in the nineteenth century, and its ruling body gained royal patronage from Edward VII, who raced pigeons himself. Elizabeth II keeps up the tradition, maintaining Royal Lofts at her Sandringham estate. The sport is most associated with working men in the north of England, some of whom put their knowledge to good effect in the First World War when thousands of pigeons were used by the Allies to send vital communications.

Allotments are small plots of land where fruit and vegetables are cultivated. They are owned municipally and tended by people who don't have their own garden. The Victorians felt that tending allotments might 'improve the moral character' of the urban poor, and soon the outskirts of towns were transformed into a patchwork of plots. What was a hobby later became vital work as the nation was exhorted to 'dig for victory' during wartime rationing.

Nowadays allotments are often the scene of intense competition between growers of **giant vegetables**. Prodigious parsnips and colossal cabbages vie for space as gardeners compete for prizes using fair methods and sometimes foul.

For those who prefer to spend their leisure time indoors, Britain is home to some of the world's finest theatres – notably in London's West End. It also offers less formal theatrical entertainments in the form of amateur dramatics, music hall and variety, and pantomime.

Many an actor's first experience of the smell of greasepaint is in **amateur dramatics** or **am-dram**. Low-budget productions in church halls often give budding thespians a taste for treading the boards and a brief non-speaking role can have even the most modest talents dreaming of the West End.

A different form of stagecraft was required for **music hall**, the most popular form of entertainment for ordinary people in the nineteenth and early twentieth centuries. Starting humbly in pubs where patrons would get up and do a 'turn' to amuse fellow drinkers, music hall then developed along professional lines and soon purpose-built halls housed paying customers who wanted to see the finest **variety** acts of the day. Household names of the music-hall era included comedian George Robey 'the Prime Minister of Mirth' and Marie Lloyd, a singer whose double entendres subjected her to the attentions of censorious 'vigilance' committees. The music hall's most famous impresario was Fred Karno. He is not well known today, but two members of his troupe went on to become Hollywood legends: Charlie Chaplin and Stan Laurel.

Music hall was killed by television, but its spirit lives on in **pantomime**, where tales such as *Peter Pan* and *Cinderella* are reworked for laughs for a family audience. A typical panto revolves around a principal boy (played by a young actress) getting the better of a pantomime dame (played by a male comedian) or a pantomime villain (ditto), while two actors combine to play a pantomime horse. Audience participation is encouraged ('he's behind you!') and productions are a highlight of the festive season.

ALL THE FUN OF THE FAIR

The calendar in the British Isles is filled with various national and local holidays, many of which are connected with fairs and festivals. Some are in rude health and others take a very different form from the original event.

❖ In English history a **mop fair** was a large gathering at which labourers without employment would seek work. People would carry one of the tools of their trade to make themselves known to potential employers. So, for example, a domestic servant would carry a mop or a broom, while a shepherd might attach a lock of wool to his hat. The fairs traditionally took place on or around Michaelmas Day. The hiring element to the fair has long since disappeared and modern versions are simply fun fairs.

❖ **Wakes** were originally religious festivals, but during the Industrial Revolution they became annual works holidays called **wakes weeks**. Each industrial town in the north of England would adopt a particular week during the summer when all the factories would shut down for a week. In the early twentieth century this meant that the North's favourite holiday resort, Blackpool, would play host to holidaymakers from a different town each week. Industrial towns in Scotland also operated this system, although north of the border the holidays are known as **fairs**.

❖ A **hopping** used to be a rural festival which had dancing as its main element. In the north-east of England the **Hoppings** is a fun fair held in Newcastle in the last week of June. The Hoppings started as a fair organized by the Temperance Movement (a body opposed to the drinking of alcohol) and coincides with a major horseracing meeting.

❖ To **beat the bounds** is an old custom, still observed in some English parishes, of going round the parish boundaries on Ascension Day at the end of the Easter period. Schoolboys, accompanied by parish officials and clergymen, walk round the boundaries which the boys beat with willow wands. It is said that sometimes the boys were also beaten so that they would not forget the boundaries in a hurry, although it is unlikely that this particular part of the ceremony is still practised.

❖ A similar custom exists in south-east Scotland, where townspeople ride around their town's boundaries on horseback. In some towns it is known as the **Common Riding**, in others the **Riding of the Marches**. The ridings usually take place on a local holiday.

❖ At the opposite end of Scotland is the archipelago of Shetland, which until the fifteenth century was part of Norway. Although it has been Scottish for over five hundred years, Shetland is proud of its Norse heritage. One manifestation of this is **Up-Helly-Aa**, an annual fire festival held at the end of January. Up-Helly-Aa means 'end of the holy days (holidays)' and the centrepiece of the festival, held in the town of Lerwick, is the burning of a Viking longship by Shetland men dressed as Vikings.

❖ Another ceremony of great vintage is **well dressing**. Also called **tap dressing**, this practice has pagan origins and was originally associated with the cult of water deities. A Whitsun ceremony, well dressing involves decorating wells and other sources of pure water with designs fashioned from flower petals, leaves, and berries. Well dressing is most associated with Derbyshire, particularly the village of Tissington, where it is first recorded in the fourteenth century.

LET'S DANCE!

The eighteenth-century writer Fanny Burney complained that dancing was 'a Barbarian exercise, and of savage origin'. Perhaps this criticism was typical of her age, but it is certainly historically inaccurate.

One of the oldest forms of dancing in the British Isles is the **Morris Dance**. This ritual folk dance involves men clad in white, wearing bells, and carrying handkerchiefs and sticks. The name, it is thought, comes from *Moorish*, the Moors being an old name for the Muslim inhabitants of North Africa. Shakespeare mentions Morris dancing as a May-Day festivity in *All's Well That Ends Well*, and this suggests that its origins are pre-Christian and linked to pagan fertility rites. Morris Dancing was revived in the twentieth century and perhaps its symbolism has been lost on a modern public who usually find it either quaint or comic.

North of the border, Scotland has its own tradition of **country dancing**, where dances are enjoyed to the accompaniment of traditional music at dances called **ceilidhs** (a Gaelic word). Here **stripping the willow** and the **eightsome reel** test the stamina of groups while the **Gay Gordons** (the Gordon Highlanders were a famous Scottish regiment in the British Army) can be relied upon to tempt couples of all ages onto the dance floor.

In the twentieth century, traditional dances took a backward step. From the 1920s Britain's public broadcaster the BBC began filling radio airtime with broadcasts of concerts from **dance halls** often located in upmarket hotels. New dances such as the foxtrot and the quickstep emerged to suit the music of the Jazz Age, although dance bands on this side of the Atlantic were noticeably less 'hot' than the American big bands of Count Basie and Duke Ellington. Nevertheless, the BBC Dance Orchestra became a national institution and its conductors, Jack Payne and Henry Hall, were household names, playing a restrained form of big-band music that largely suited British tastes.

Occasionally a novelty dance would take the dance halls by storm and challenge what *The Times* called the 'tyranny of the foxtrot'. One such dance was the **Lambeth Walk**, created to publicize the musical *Me and My Girl*. This walking dance, inspired by the Cockney culture of London's East End, was a hit with everyone – even, it is said, King George VI and Queen Elizabeth (the present Queen's parents). Less pleased with the dance were the Nazis who claimed that it was 'Jewish mischief' and disliked its 'animalistic hopping'. The British Ministry of Information got wind of this and outraged Nazi high command by making a film in which the Lambeth Walk was played over footage of goose-stepping German soldiers.

Not long after the war, the BBC resumed television broadcasts and one of the earliest programmes it showed was *Come Dancing*, where British regions competed against each other in **ballroom dancing**. The show aired on and off for nearly fifty years, audiences delighting in watching couples tango, samba, and paso doble their way around the dance floor while a voiceover remarked that every sequin on their outfits had been hand-stitched. The programme came to an end in 1998, but the format was rebooted a few years later as celebrities took to the floor partnered by professional dancers. *Strictly Come Dancing* was born.

This show follows the emotional and often tearful 'journeys' of celebrities as they progress towards semi-competence, with one or two competitors chosen specifically for their flat-footed ineptitude. *Strictly*, as its fans call it, is one the BBC's biggest recent hits and has been exported to many other countries as *Dancing with the Stars*.

BEER AND SKITTLES

'Few things are more pleasant than a village graced with a good church, a good priest, and a good pub'. While some might disagree about the middle item on travel writer John Hillaby's list of essentials for a perfect village, few Britons will argue about the third. Here we ask for the 'best of order' as all things pub-related (apart, mercifully, from the **pub bore**) are celebrated. Cheers!

The word **pub** is simply a shortening of **public house**, a term which was noted just over two hundred years ago. The **publican** either owns the pub or runs it for a brewery. In the latter case the pub is a **tied house** which has to serve only the brewery's beers with, if you're lucky, a **guest ale** from another brewery.

Pubs are the traditional home of the working man relaxing after a hard day's work. Pubs with only basic comforts are referred to as '**spit and sawdust**' places, while at the other extreme the upmarket **gastropub** offers quality food and drink to clients who want something more than crisps and pork scratchings.

Features common to many pubs include the **public bar**, where the majority of drinkers enjoy their ale standing up or perched on stools, and a **saloon bar**, a separate area where furnishings are more luxurious and the drinks are slightly more expensive. Some pubs even have a third area – the **snug** – a small but comfortable room originally called the **snuggery**.

An object that might be seen behind the counter in some traditional pubs is a long drinking vessel which, when filled with two or three pints of beer, is called the **yard of ale**. Drinking its contents in one go is an act of bravado reserved normally for rugby-playing types and not for beer connoisseurs.

More discerning drinkers usually sit quietly in the snug nursing pints of real ale, desperate to avoid boisterous younger drinkers who might be in the middle of a **pub crawl**. This activity involves going to a number of different pubs within the same area and having a drink (or two) at each one. In Glasgow there is a variation of this called the **sub crawl** where participants have a drink in a pub near to every one of the city's fifteen subway (underground-railway) stations.

Pub games are a feature of many old-fashioned pubs and in the games room you might find **bar billiards**, a game resembling **pool** but which features wooden pegs, a table without any corner and side pockets, and a set of rules that mystifies the average pub goer.

A simpler game is **shove ha'penny**, where coins are perched on the end of a table then propelled by the palm of one's hand across a marked board. More exciting is **darts**, where players throw small sharp metal projectiles at a round board divided into numbered beds. Darts is good to play but also fun to watch – so much so that the sport is now played by professionals and televised. The traditional games have their adherents, but for the modern 'pub athlete' the '**pub triathlon**' consists of pool, darts, and **dominoes**.

Before recent legislation, pubs had to observe strict opening hours. The final pub rituals of the evening were enacted towards 11pm, when 'Last orders' was announced and drinkers raced to get a final 'swift half' before a bell was rung and the barman called, 'Time gentlemen please!' This marked '**chucking out time**' and the pub was emptied of its drinkers, the more literate of whom might recall the words of the Reverend Sydney Smith: 'What two ideas are more inseparable than beer and Britannia?'

DOWN AT THE OLD BULL AND BUSH

Visitors to public houses must sometimes wonder why the hostelry in which they are imbibing has such an unusual name. A country pub called the 'Plough and Harrow' needs no explanation but what about the '**Royal Oak**' or the '**Lamb and Flag**'? Put your glass down for a minute as we consider the names commonly found on signs outside British pubs.

Animals are often to be found gracing pub signs and two very common names are the '**White Hart**' and the '**White Horse**'. The first is a deer that sometimes sports a golden chain and is the badge of fourteenth-century English monarch Richard II. He insisted that public houses display a sign and for a time the White Hart was *the* symbol of ale houses. The 'White Horse' is a symbol of the House of Hanover who took over from the Stuarts as Britain's Royal House in 1714. It is also the symbol of the county of Kent.

The '**Red Lion**' is the most ubiquitous pub name in Britain. It is a common symbol of coats of arms so there is no one single origin. Depending on the pub, it may symbolize the royal arms of Scotland and England following the succession of the Stuarts in 1603, or it could refer to the founder of the House of Lancaster, John of Gaunt. Or it may just be a symbol of some forgotten local landowner.

Other names with royal connections include the '**Rose and Crown**', a common pub name in England. Dynastic conflicts called the Wars of the Roses between the House of York (symbolized by a white rose) and the House of Lancaster (which adopted a red rose) were fought in the fifteenth century. The conflict was settled and the roses combined into the red-and-white rose of the new ruling house, the Tudors. This rose, often crowned, is a symbol of the monarchy of England.

The '**Royal Oak**' refers to a famous tree in English history, the one in which Charles II hid when he fled Oliver Cromwell's army after the Battle of Worcester in 1651. Charles went into exile but eventually returned to England and the monarchy was restored after a brief period of republican rule.

Royal symbols abound in pub signs but religious ones are also common. The '**Lamb and Flag**' shows a lamb holding a flag and this is a representation of Christ's resurrection, the 'Lamb of God' being a name for Jesus. The flag shows a red cross on a white background and this later became England's national flag. The '**Cross Keys**' is another name with religious imagery and in this case the cross keys are the sign of St Peter, the 'Gatekeeper of Heaven'. A pub with this name might be found near a church dedicated to the saint.

Historic events are frequently celebrated in pub signs. The enemies of the Christian Crusaders in medieval times are remembered in the '**Turk's Head**' and the '**Saracen's Head**', while the '**Olde Trip to Jerusalem**' in Nottingham claims to be England's oldest pub and a point of departure for the Crusades.

Also in Nottinghamshire is the '**Cuckoo Bush**' which derives its name from a local legend where some simple rustic types thought they could prolong summer by preventing a cuckoo from flying off.

Our final stop is the '**Green Man**'. An ancient symbol, Green Men can be found decorating some medieval churches, where their heads are wreathed in foliage. He is believed to be a pagan deity adopted by the Church as a symbol of Easter and resurrection, although not all who have looked into the matter see him as benevolent.

GAME FOR ANYTHING

Britain is the birthplace of many of the world's favourite competitive activities. There are, however, a number of games that have yet to be taken up by the rest of the world. It is these games, some from the playground, others played at certain schools, and still others restricted to a particular town, that we will now tackle.

Schoolchildren nowadays might spend their breaks texting and tweeting but older generations will remember a time when the playground was a noisy scene of informal games. One game, now more likely to be played only by adults, is **conkers**. A conker is the fruit of the horse chestnut tree threaded on a string, and the game involves swinging it against another player's conker with the intention of smashing it. Conkers are judged, like boxers, on the number of opponents they have seen off, so a conker with six victories is known as a 'sixer'. But if a sixer breaks a 'twelver' it takes possession of its vanquished opponent's wins and becomes a 'nineteener'. The word 'conker', incidentally, comes from a dialect word for the snail shells originally used in the game.

Another fondly remembered playground game is **British Bulldog**. This is where one player standing in the middle of the playground tries to catch opposing players as they attempt to run to the other side. If caught, a player joins the player in the middle, and the game continues until everyone is caught. The game is like rugby played without a ball and, like that game, involves the sort of rough physicality now discouraged by teachers nervous of litigious parents.

Rough physicality is still encouraged at our public schools, the most famous of which, Eton, is known for two games. **Fives** is similar to squash but played with gloved hands rather than racquets, and **Eton Fives** is played in a three-walled court while a four-walled court is used by Eton's rival public schools, Rugby and Winchester. More infamous is the **Eton wall game**, a curious contest in which a seemingly endless loose scrum takes place against a wall in a field. Scoring is rare, indeed no goals have been scored in the annual St Andrew's Day match since 1909. Winchester also has a football-type game, known informally as **Winkies**, while the ball game played at Harrow is referred to as **footer**.

Even older are the medieval **mob football** games still played in various towns across the British Isles. Intra-town rivalry is a feature and the '**uppies**' often take on the '**downies**' (or '**doonies**' in Scotland). Games are usually annual and played on a traditional holiday such as Shrove Tuesday. A similar game is played in Cornwall called **hurling the silver ball**.

At the other end of the country is another traditional sport: **tossing the caber**. A feature of Scottish Highland games, this requires the thrower to pick up a **caber** (Gaelic for 'pole') and throw it so that it lands away from the thrower on its heavy end.

This game is safe for spectators, assuming they stand well away from the action, unlike our next sport: **cheese rolling**. Put simply, cheese rolling involves people running down a steep hill in hot pursuit of a giant disc of cheese. An annual tradition in Gloucestershire, home of Double Gloucester cheese, injuries are common and ambulances always on standby.

Less dangerous but no less silly is **bog snorkelling**, an aquatic contest recently devised in Wales. A narrow, shallow stretch of muddy water in Llanwrtyd Wells is traversed twice by swimmers in snorkels and flippers. Like so many good ideas the sport emerged from a conversation in a pub.

GOOD SPORTS!

Britain has made numerous contributions to mankind's well-being in science, medicine, and engineering. But for millions of people it is for inventing and exporting many of the world's most popular sports that Britain deserves thanks. Here we take a look at why Britain is the 'home' of so many sports.

George Orwell famously wrote that sport is 'war minus the shooting'. He was certainly right about the sports popular in the past with royalty and nobility. Hunting was *the* sport for the upper classes and until relatively recently a 'sportsman' was simply another word for someone who enjoyed hunting.

In the eighteenth century the enclosure of common land into private plots resulted in walls, hedges, and fences being put up. Horsemen found that leaping those obstacles was rather fun and soon **steeplechasing** became a sport. The descendents of the Arab horses brought back from the crusades in the twelfth century began to be raced on purpose-built courses such as Newmarket (still known among the turf fraternity as 'headquarters'), and the sport was given royal patronage by Charles II and Queen Anne. The '**classic**' English horse races, such as the **Derby**, became established and aristocrats won and lost fortunes on gambling.

The following century was altogether more sober. Rakish aristocrats had fallen out of favour as the middle classes grew in strength during the Industrial Revolution. Sports needed to be 'character building' if Britain's Empire was to be maintained. Public schools felt duty-bound to create future Empire builders by teaching their young charges teamwork, selflessness, and fair play.

For this, new team sports were needed. The Victorians took the primitive ball games that had been played for centuries and gave them structure. **Rugby** (named after the school from which it perhaps originated) and **football** (soccer) emerged in the mid-nineteenth century along with the ruling bodies that governed them. More sports soon followed in this vein.

Sport was by no means restricted to public schools. Working people, who had campaigned for shorter working hours, needed recreation on their weekends off and were soon paying at the gate to see professional football. More genteel sports were required for the middle classes and **golf**, hitherto restricted to Scotland, spread throughout the British Isles as the growing railway network made it easier to get to the nation's mainly '**links**' (seaside) courses. The first **Open** golf championship was played in 1860 and golf, once banned by James II of Scotland, got royal patronage and the game's ruling body in St Andrews was given the title **Royal and Ancient**.

Lawn **tennis**, pioneered by Walter Wingfield and initially having the Greek name *sphairistike*, also became popular among the middle classes. **Cricket**'s popularity was more widespread and was exported to the Empire and an intense rivalry with Australia quickly grew. The export of sports to the Empire wasn't all one way, however. Bored British Army officers serving in India created the game of **snooker** and it soon returned to the 'mother country', while **polo** (an ancient Asian sport) was imported by cavalry officers to Britain where its ruling body, the **Hurlingham Club**, was founded.

Other sports for which Victorian Britain drew up rules include **table tennis**, **badminton** (named after Badminton Hall, seat of the Dukes of Beaufort), and **squash**. **Boxing**, once little better than brawling, was given rules endorsed by the Marquess of Queensberry in the 1860s, while **athletics** and **swimming** also established governing bodies and their first championships.

Britain gave the world so many sports, yet the world repays us by beating Britain more often than not. Just as well it's the playing and not the winning that matters!

THE PLACE TO BE

The British sporting calendar has a number of traditional fixtures, and many places have become closely identified with the sports that are played there. The meetings at Ascot, Cowes, and Henley in particular are regarded as fixed points of the annual '**season**' of summer social events for members of fashionable society.

❖ **Aintree** is a racecourse in Liverpool and home to Britain's most celebrated steeplechase, the **Grand National**. The race, run each spring, comprises two circuits totalling four and a half miles with jumps that have to be negotiated twice. Its most famous jump, **Becher's Brook**, is named after Captain Martin Becher who in 1839 parted company from his mount and was flung into the brook that eventually bore his name. He is said to have remarked 'how dreadful water tastes without the benefit of whisky'.

❖ Ascot is a racecourse near Windsor, founded in 1711 by Queen Anne. It is home to the **Royal Ascot** meeting. The meeting is a highlight of the 'flat' season (where horses race without having to negotiate fences), but many female spectators attend merely to show off their dresses and hats, especially on **Ladies' Day**. The Queen, a great follower of the 'sport of kings', graces the **Royal Enclosure** where a strict dress code is enforced.

❖ Cowes is a port on the Isle of Wight and is England's most celebrated yachting centre. The annual **Cowes Regatta** has been held here, organized by the Royal Yacht Squadron, since 1776. **Cowes Week** (in the first week of August) is the climax of the yachting season.

❖ Henley-on-Thames in Oxfordshire is the home of the **Henley Royal Regatta**, the oldest rowing regatta in Europe. The regatta has been held annually since 1839 and won its 'Royal' prefix in 1851 when Prince Albert patronized the event. Aside from top-class rowing the Regatta is famed for its lawn parties, especially those in the exclusive **Stewards' Enclosure** where boating blazers and straw hats are *de rigueur* for men and frocks of the appropriate length are required for the ladies.

❖ **Silverstone** is a motor-racing circuit in Northamptonshire. It was built on the site of a wartime airfield and is most famous for hosting the first Grand Prix of the inaugural Formula One World Drivers' Championship in 1950. In 1987, after several decades of alternating with **Brands Hatch**, Silverstone became the permanent home of the **British Grand Prix**.

❖ **St Andrews** is a town in Fife in Scotland and is regarded as the **Home of Golf**. The sport has been played here since the middle ages and the town is home to the **Royal and Ancient Golf Club**, the game's ruling body (except in the US). St Andrews' most famous course is the **Old Course** which has hosted golf's premier championship, **the Open**, many times. The course is famed for its huge double greens and includes holes with charming names such as 'Ginger Beer' and 'Heathery'.

❖ **Wimbledon** is a district of south-west London and home to the **Wimbledon Championships**, tennis's only Grand Slam tournament still played on grass. Run by the **All England Lawn Tennis and Croquet Club**, the Championships (played since 1877) are a part of the sporting and social summer season. The club has numerous courts, the largest of which is **Centre Court** (now with a movable roof to avoid rain delays), where British fans eat strawberries and cream while hoping (usually forlornly) for British success.

FOOTBALL CRAZY

'Football without fans is nothing,' said the Scottish football manager Jock Stein. Few would disagree as the 'beautiful game' would be an unremarkable spectacle without the noise, colour, and passion of the fans.

The first people to watch football were more spectators than fans. They turned up at muddy fields out of curiosity to see the new sport of **association football** and wondered why players weren't allowed to handle the ball and who on earth came up with the **offside** rule.

Once the game developed and every town in the country got itself a team or two, local rivalries emerged. The **Derby** was the most famous horserace of the day but soon the new sport had appropriated the name and even before the First World War fans started to call matches between neighbouring teams **derbies**. Local derbies became and still are more important than other matches and 'bragging rights' (a modern phrase but not a modern phenomenon) were won and lost.

Other conventions that eventually became time-honoured traditions were the **three o'clock kick-off** and the **half-time** break after which the teams changed ends. As club loyalties developed, fans wanted to differentiate themselves from supporters of other clubs and started to wear scarves and hats in the colours of their team. It was natural to want to congregate with one's fellow fans, and so supporters started to assemble at different 'ends' of the ground. The tradition of '**home**' and '**away**' supporters had begun.

Newspapers were quick to cash in on football's popularity. Reports of matches appeared in the back pages, and photographs of games were used in '**spot the ball**' competitions. League tables were published and these were probably used to assist participants in football's new betting craze of the 1920s: **football pools**.

Fans were keen to give as much support to their team as possible. As well as appropriately coloured scarves and hats, the **football rattle** was a noisy – but mercifully short-lived – method of generating supportive decibels. Lyrics, often to the tune of popular songs and even hymns, were written and sung before, during, and after games. Chants, supportive for one's own team and derisive of the opposition, were also in evidence and some (usually ones disputing his parentage) were even reserved for the referee.

Memorabilia was, and still is, keenly collected and many a fan's cupboard has been filled with match programmes, badges, cigarette cards bearing players' faces, and even old ticket stubs that they can't quite bring themselves to throw away.

In the modern era some fans express affection for their club by starting a **fanzine**, a rough-and-ready independent pamphlet that is usually irreverent and sometimes critical of the current players, manager, or owners. The fanzine might also take a dig at fellow fans, especially the sort derided as **glory-hunters**, who only turn up when the team is winning. Diehard fans are characterized as relishing half-time fare of pies and **Bovril**, in contrast to the fair-weather supporters in corporate boxes, who have been dubbed the **prawn-sandwich brigade**.

For many fans the game does not end with the final whistle. Disputed penalties and inept performances must be discussed not just with fellow fans but with the entire nation, or at least with the listeners of one of football's newest traditions, the **football phone-in**. These shows allow fans, often standing in motorway service stations and shaking with rage, to bellow down their phones to a pundit in a studio. Internet message boards and social networking keep the debate going so that football fans, instead of indulging their passion only when Saturday comes, can now enjoy it round the clock.

IF YOU'LL PARDON THE CLICHÉ

Football is a source of air-punching joy and complete despair, an ever-changing, spellbinding saga. Unfortunately, when players, managers, and commentators get talking about it they are rarely able to do so without resorting to clichés, many of which are either self-evident or complete gibberish. Here is a selection of the worst offenders:

❖ A good time to score *When isn't it?*

❖ He's got a great touch for a big man *Yet no-one says 'rubbish touch for a small man'.*

❖ He's in acres of space *No, he's not.*

❖ He knows where the goal is *Well done him!*

❖ He's literally run his socks off *Looks like they're still on him from here.*

❖ He struck that shot too well *Silly boy.*

❖ It's a must-win game *Those 'must-lose' games are really dull.*

❖ It's a shame that one team had to lose *Failing to get to get to grips with the essential nature of sport.*

❖ It's important we get off to a good start *Unlike the other times when an awful start would be fine.*

❖ That's a bad time to concede a goal *So should they have waited a bit longer and then let it in?*

❖ The keeper made himself big *Isn't that cheating?*

❖ This team is too good to go down *But not good enough to be able to keep itself up…*

❖ We are taking it one game at a time *Unlike those idiots that take it two games at a time, eh?*

When football fans get together it is only a matter of time before a favourite anthem or chant is belted out in unison. Some songs date to the old days of the music hall, others might take inspiration from a recent pop song. Some are celebratory, others ironic, and still more are slanderous attacks on rival teams. Here are some of the most distinctive songs that you might hear at British grounds:

36-nil, 36-nil, hello, hello: a reminder by Arbroath fans of the side's triumph over Bon Accord in the 1885 Scottish Cup. The score is a British senior record and unlikely ever to be beaten.

Good old Arsenal: the traditional song of England's 'establishment' club, released as a single by the 1971 squad who won a famous league and cup double.

Oh they should have built a wall and not a bridge: sung by Bristol Rovers fans in reference to the Severn Bridge that links Bristol to Wales, home of rivals Cardiff City and Swansea.

We only sing when we're fishing: an ironic reworking of the classic *You only sing when you're winning* taunt, sung by followers of Grimsby Town in allusion to the chief local industry.

Don't cry for me, Boston United: Lloyd Webber and Rice's famous lament from *Evita* reworded by supporters of Lincoln City to fan the flames of Lincolnshire rivalry.

The Blaydon Races: a mid-nineteenth-century song referring to a celebrated horse-racing meeting, it is the unofficial anthem of Newcastle United and is also sung by supporters of Newcastle Falcons rugby club.

We're not Scousers, we're from Birkenhead: a defiant geographical reminder from fans of Tranmere Rovers that their team has *nothing whatsoever* to do with Liverpool.

Hark now hear the Walsall sing: a classic Christmas carol reworded by supporters of the West Midlands club – it's what the tune's composer, Felix Mendelssohn, would have wanted.

FLANNELLED FOOLS

The game of cricket has humble rural origins deep in England's past where a rudimentary version of the game was played by bored shepherds with their crooks. It developed into a more familiar form in the eighteenth century when eleven-a-side matches became standard and local rivalries emerged. A set of rules was drawn up in 1774 then revised by the game's first ruling body, the **Marylebone Cricket Club** (**MCC**), in 1788.

The game evolved at pace in the nineteenth century. The cricket ground of **Lord's** (named after ex-player Thomas Lord) was established at St John's Wood in London and it quickly became the game's headquarters. **Test matches** (long games between national teams) started in the 1870s and a famous win by Australia at London's other major ground, the **Oval**, in 1882 was so lamented that the 'death of English cricket' was announced by one newspaper and the ashes of the ceremonially burnt stumps and bails were put in a small urn. Thus began one of the oldest rivalries in sport: **the Ashes**.

In this century, and beyond, British public schools considered sport to be the ideal preparation for both war and life in general. Sporting behaviour and abiding by the rules meant everything. In cricket this spirit was summed up in two phrases: '**playing with a straight bat**', (which has become a byword for correct behaviour) and '**not cricket**' which describes anything underhand.

One of cricket's appeals at this time was that it allowed different classes to mix. Indeed, historian GM Trevelyan observed that 'if the French noblesse had been capable of playing cricket with their peasants, their chateaux would never have been burnt'. Cricket might have prevented class conflict but class differences were still closely observed and the distinction between **Players** (professionals) and **Gentlemen** (those wealthy enough to play for fun) lasted well into the twentieth century.

Strangers to cricket are often amazed that a match lasting five days can end in a draw. They might also observe the numerous stoppages for lunch, tea, drinks, rain, and bad light and concur with English churchman William Temple that cricket is nothing more than 'organized loafing'. Spectators of the '**timeless tests**' of the pre-war era, when some matches went on as long as ten days, might well have agreed with this assessment.

Attempts to dispel this image came after World War II in the form of **one-day cricket** where a limited number of overs guaranteed a result and reversed the trend of dwindling crowds. This was also the era where Britain's ex-colonies attempted to get one over their old masters. Rivalries could get intense, especially between England and an Australian side who refuse to forget the controversial 1932–33 '**Bodyline**' tour where England's aggressive bowling led to a diplomatic incident.

Not every cricket lover can get to a test match but he or she can still enjoy the game through the medium of radio. In Britain, the BBC's **Test Match Special** (affectionately known as 'TMS') covers important matches and has become an institution in its own right. The eccentricities of its commentators, their fondness for cakes sent in by listeners, and the tension of missing several minutes of a game while coverage is broken for the **shipping forecast** make TMS unmissable for many.

The newest form of cricket is **Twenty20** where a game can be crammed into three hours and Indian billionaires bid in auctions for the world's top stars to play in their teams. Bollywood glamour has been added as cricket's centre of power has shifted east, but the game is still, by and large, quintessentially English and reassuringly old-fashioned.

SHORT, SQUARE, AND SILLY

When a team takes its turn to field in a game of cricket its job is to stop the batting team from scoring runs. It does this by putting its fielders in certain positions where it thinks the batsman is likely to hit the ball.

The fielding team has eleven players, one who bowls the ball (the bowler) and one who stands at all times behind the wicket (the wicketkeeper). The remaining nine players may be placed in various positions around the field of play. Each position has a name, but the position's name can vary according to how close it is to the batsman or what angle it is to the batsman's crease.

Still paying attention? Understanding the following terms should make things clearer...

- ❖ The **off side** is the area to the right of a right-handed batsman or to the left of a left-handed batsman; the **on side** or **leg side** is the area to the left of a right-handed batsman or to the right of a left-handed batsman.

- ❖ A position that is **deep** or **long** is further from the batsman than normal; a position called **short** is nearer the batsman than normal; while **silly** means dangerously near the batsman.

- ❖ A position that is **wide** is at a larger angle to the line of the pitch, whereas a position that is **fine** is at a shorter angle to the line of the pitch.

- ❖ A position that is **square** is along an imaginary line level with the batsman's crease; **backward** means behind the batsman's crease; **forward** means in front of the batman's crease.

- ❖ A fielder who is **straight** is positioned close to an imaginary line along the middle of the pitch between the two sets of stumps.

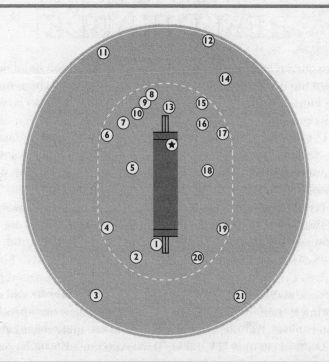

Cricket fielding positions

1. bowler
2. mid off
3. long off
4. cover
5. silly mid off
6. point
7. gully
8. slips
9. slips
10. slips
11. third man
12. long leg
13. wicket keeper
14. fine leg
15. leg slip
16. short leg
17. square leg
18. silly mid off
19. midwicket
20. mid on
21. long on
★ batsman (right-handed batsman)

QUITE
REMARKABLE!

Live sports commentary is a tricky business. Mistakes cannot be edited out nor can gaffes be discarded on the cutting room floor. The satirical magazine *Private Eye* delights in such howlers and prints them in its '**Colemanballs**' column, named in honour of David Coleman. Resorting to stock phrases is a temptation for broadcasters, but avoiding them is easier said than done. On this page we celebrate Britain's favourite commentators, the phrases they coined, and the slip-ups that left them red-faced.

David Coleman's career as an athletics commentator for the BBC was celebrated with the award of the Olympic Order, the movement's highest honour. His commentaries, however, did not always reach Olympian heights. One gaffe attributed to him involved Cuban runner Alberto Juantorena who 'just opened his legs wide and showed us all his class'. In a similar vein he said of a sprinter: 'Linford Christie has a habit of pulling it out when it matters most'. As Coleman himself used to say: **quite remarkable!**

On rival channel ITV, Dickie Davies was normally unflappable but one Saturday the anchorman let slip an unfortunate Spoonerism. Instead of introducing 'cup soccer' he promised an afternoon of 'cop sucker'. This was a rare but regrettable mistake for Dickie, in stark contrast to the utterances of football summarizer Ron Atkinson. Atkinson, a former defender, tackled English in the way he used to tackle forwards: wholeheartedly but without much style. His abuses of the language became known as '**Ronglish**' and his major contribution to the pantheon of clichés is '**early doors**' (as in 'United will be disappointed to concede early doors').

Football, Atkinson might concede, is a '**funny old game**'. This oft-said remark is most associated with Jimmy Greaves, an ex-player turned pundit who teamed up with Scotsman Ian St John in the 1980s to dispense similar nuggets of soccer wisdom on *The Saint & Greavsie Show*.

Football is enjoyed throughout the country but rugby league was mainly confined to the north of England until Eddie Waring came along. A former team manager and sports journalist, he was perfect to promote the game from behind the microphone in the 1960s and 1970s. His enthusiasm and unusual vocal style made him a household name and gems such as '**up-and-under**' (a steepling kick) and '**early bath**' (what a player enjoys when he is sent off for foul play) are fondly remembered.

Equally fondly remembered is Bill McLaren who became the voice of rugby union during the same time. McLaren, a Scot from the Borders, was keen on agricultural metaphors. Flankers were compared to charging bulls and a hefty forward would be described as 'nineteen stones on the hoof'. Scampering centres might perform a '**shilly-shally**' to evade a tackler, foul play was '**jiggery-pokery**', and brawls '**argy-bargy**'.

Broadcasting legends abound in cricket and most have worked for the BBC's *Test Match Special*. TMS commentators are relaxed enough to enjoy a gaffe. When a batsman hit his own wicket because 'he couldn't get his leg over', Brian Johnston dissolved into laughter. The subsequent few minutes became part of broadcasting history and the recording has even been requested on that other British institution *Desert Island Discs*.

Fast-moving sports are prone to commentator gaffes but more sedate ones can also fall foul. In the early days of snooker, colour television was also in its infancy and Ted Lowe, attempting to help viewers, ended up confusing everyone by remarking 'for those of you watching in black and white, the pink is behind the green'.

And finally we arrive at the legendary, Murray Walker. The BBC's motor racing commentator for five decades, Walker's classic Colemanballs are legion. Here is one as good as any: 'Rene Arnoux is coming into the pits ... let's stop the startwatch'.

FOOD
AND
DRINK

THE BRITISH DIET

Historically, the British people have never had much of a clue when it comes to food. It has been said that while other nations live to eat, the British merely eat to live. Certainly, many a visitor to these islands has had an unpleasant surprise when presented with a plate of fatty meat swimming in thick gravy or a pudding of indeterminate nature doused with congealing custard.

Perhaps the traditionally stodgy British diet has developed as a result of the country's cool and wet climate. It is certainly true that a good dose of carbohydrates provides us with an extra layer of defence to ward off the chill of winter. Nevertheless, there have been concerns about the effect that traditional eating habits have had on the national health, especially in our chillier northern regions. The city of Glasgow has been dubbed the 'heart-attack capital of Europe', a situation not helped by the fondness of the natives to dip everything into a deep-fat fryer before eating it – not just battered fish, but even pizzas and chocolate bars!

However, the stereotype of Britain as a food-lovers' hell is now surely becoming outdated. The country is falling in love with good food and we all want to learn how to prepare it for our family and friends. Television abounds with cookery shows, many of them fronted by a 'celebrity chef' whose mission is to enlighten the country about a particular style of cooking. The recommendation of a particular ingredient by one of these chefs can see it disappear from the supermarket shelves in huge volumes! Moreover, we have not been shy about adopting the cuisines of other nations: where once a British takeaway meal meant fish and chips, nowadays our high streets offer Italian, Indian, Chinese, Mexican, and Thai food almost as a matter of course, and many other cuisines can be found in our larger cities.

In this part of the book, we are proud to offer a menu of fine British food. We look at some of the dishes that have been developed as local delicacies in different parts of the country. The geographical diversity of British food is in fact a recurring theme, and many areas offer their own versions of dishes, each varying according to the local ingredients and traditions, and usually each with its own local name. The different types of bread are a good example of this: you might ask for a 'buttery' in Aberdeen, but don't expect them to understand what this is in Cardiff!

For our main course, we tuck into some of the nation's favourite pies, before taking a bite out of some savoury and sweet puddings. It is now that the famous British 'sweet tooth' really comes into its own, as we consider the myriad types of cakes, sweets, and biscuits that are available in Britain's tea shops and which keep the nation's dentists in full employment.

After the sweet trolley has been removed we linger over the cheeseboard, observing how the names of many places in Britain have entered the language through the foods that are produced there. And, of course, after such a cornucopia of food we need something to help us wash it down. So we will round off this particular feast with a look at the nation's favourite tipples, considering the tradition of British brewing and also the Scottish national drink of whisky.

It's quite amazing that a nation with a reputation for culinary ineptitude should have come up with so many mouth-watering dishes, and the sheer variety of our local delicacies has certainly helped to provide the English language with some curious and evocative words!

THE LOCAL
SPECIALITY

Although Britain is a relatively small country, it is geographically and regionally diverse. Here we look at how this diversity is reflected in some of our traditional dishes.

The writer William Somerset Maugham claimed that 'to eat well in England you should have breakfast three times a day'. He was referring to the cooked breakfast of bacon, eggs, sausage, and fried bread, but he did not note that each of the home nations has its own variation. In Scotland they favour **square sausage** (also called **Lorne sausage**), sliced from a rectangular block, while **potato scones** are preferred to fried bread. Over in Northern Ireland the **Ulster Fry** is similarly hearty but carbohydrates come in the form of **farls**, triangular sections of **soda bread**, or **boxty** (potato bread). An English breakfast may include **bubble-and-squeak** (cooked cabbage and potato fried together, so-called because of the noise it makes while cooking) or a **Cumberland sausage**, a long strip of sausage meat cooked in a spiral. In Wales, however, you may be served **laver bread** ('Welshman's caviar'), where boiled seaweed is puréed and then fried in oatmeal. The 'full Welsh' might also be served with a **Glamorgan sausage**, which is made from cheese rather than pork.

Cheese is also to be found in another dish from the Principality, the ultimate in cheese on toast: **Welsh rabbit** or **rarebit**. The national symbol of Wales is the **leek**, a vegetable to be found in many dishes, while **hill lamb** is another source of Welsh culinary pride.

Across the Irish Sea, soft rains and rich soil are ideal for growing vegetables. In Northern Ireland, **potato and parsley soup** is a winter staple while boiled ham will often be served with mashed potato. **Champ** is mashed potato with spring onions, while **colcannon**, mash mixed with kale or cabbage, is so celebrated it even has its own folk song.

In Scotland, leftover potatoes and meat are stewed together to make **stovies**, while **bashit neeps** and **tatties** (mashed turnip and potato) are the accompaniments to **haggis**. The haggis is not, as some Scots might tell the tourists, a small creature that roams Scottish hillsides, but a dish made from the 'pluck' (heart, liver, and lungs) of a sheep minced with oatmeal, suet, and spices and traditionally cooked in a sheep's stomach. It is served at a **Burns Supper**, held every January to commemorate Scotland's national poet Robert Burns who called haggis the 'great chieftain o' the puddin'-race'.

The great chieftain of the pudding race in Lancashire is **black pudding**, a blood sausage served sliced. One town closely associated with the dish is Bury, which hosts that noted annual athletic event, the World Black Pudding Throwing Championship. In nearby Wigan is a similarly important contest, the World Pie Eating Championship, where native Wiganers, known as 'Pie Eaters', are usually the favourites. Their moniker derives from 1926 when striking Wigan miners 'ate humble pie' as they returned to work. The county is also home to **Lancashire hotpot**, a stew made from lamb and onions with a crispy top of sliced potatoes.

In London, the eel plays a role in a two famous dishes. **Jellied eels** is a pub favourite, while **pie and mash** is served with a sauce, or 'liquor', made from stewed eels.

We end our culinary tour of Britain in England's southwest, where the **cream tea** is a scone served with **clotted cream** and jam. The **Devonshire tea** has cream first then the jam, while the **Cornish cream tea** has the cream dolloped on top of the jam. The order of the toppings is a source of great disputation between the two counties.

OUR DAILY BREAD

It is said that man cannot live by bread alone, although anyone familiar with the wealth of baked goods to be had in the British Isles might disagree. Here we look at the breads, savoury and sweet, that are our 'staff of life'.

The simple charms of one of Britain's favourite breads – baked in two round lumps, the smaller on top – were not lost on George Orwell who opined, 'If there is anything quite as good as the soft part of the crust from an English **cottage loaf** I do not know of it.'

Orwell, the author of *The Road to Wigan Pier*, might also have been familiar with **barm cakes**, a speciality of north-west England. A round flat soft roll, the barm cake (from an old word meaning 'yeast') is a constituent of that classic Northern combination of calories and carbohydrates, the **chip butty**.

The **stottie cake** occupies a similar place in the diet of England's north-east. A flat round loaf cut into wedges (**stotties**), this bread is usually split and crammed with a filling.

North of the border is the **potato scone**, a thin triangular scone often fried and served with a full Scottish breakfast. In north-east Scotland no breakfast is complete without a **rowie** or **buttery**. This flaky roll, as the name suggests, has a salty, buttery taste that the people of Aberdeen find hard to resist. The **bannock**, a round, flat unsweetened cake made from barley or oats and cooked on a griddle, is another Scottish favourite.

The bannock is a relative of **soda bread** (or **wheaten bread**) which is a staple across the Irish Sea where it is sometimes quartered into **farls** (an old Scots word) then fried and served with that delicious but waist-expanding breakfast the Ulster fry.

There is also no shortage of baked goods of a more sugary nature. In Ireland comes a tea-time treat called **barmbrack**. The name is Gaelic and means 'speckled loaf', a reference to the currants and candied peel in the dough. A Halloween tradition in Ireland involves concealing a ring in the baking mixture; whoever finds the ring, goes the tradition, will be the first to marry.

A bread with a similar name hails from Wales. **Bara brith** (Welsh for 'speckled loaf') has dough that contains caraway seeds and dried vine fruits. In the south of the Principality it is also known as **teisen dorth** (loaf cake).

The word 'bun' first appeared in English in 1371 in a text prescribing the weights and sizes of baked goods. Since then, England has been the capital of the bun world, and some of its creations have become known beyond the British Isles.

Most famous of all is the **hot cross bun**. The eating of spiced buns at Easter dates to Tudor times but it perhaps wasn't until the eighteenth century that they appeared with a Christian cross scored into them. Evidence of the famous street cry 'one-a-penny, two-a-penny, hot cross buns' also dates to this time – as does the practice of serving them hot.

The **Chelsea bun** first appears in the writings of satirist Jonathan Swift. Named after a fashionable London district, they were said to be favourites of George III and Queen Charlotte.

Another popular bun of the era was the **Bath bun**, named after the elegant city in the West Country. The original bun, although studded with raisins and candied peel, had a light dough. Later versions got heavier, and perhaps the author Jane Austen had sampled a stodgier version when she admitted in her diary that she had been 'disordering my Stomach with Bath bunns'.

WHO ATE ALL
THE PIES?

Although pies exist in many cuisines, the word 'pie' itself is unique to English where mystery surrounds its origin. There is a theory that it derives from an early name for the magpie (from the Latin *pica*), and that the putting together of the various ingredients of a pie was reminiscent of a magpie's habit of collecting objects to make its nest. Whatever the explanation, pies have been a part of the British diet for many years with almost every region having its own speciality.

From Cornwall, for example, we have not one but two pies. One is popular throughout Britain, the other more of a local speciality. The striking **stargazey pie**, traditionally eaten before Christmas, gets its name from the whole fish whose heads protrude from the crust. If the prospect of going eyeball to eyeball with your dinner does not appeal to you then perhaps the **Cornish pasty** will be more to your liking. Made from short pastry and filled with diced skirt of beef and potatoes, onions, and turnips, this pie was originally intended as a 'meal in itself' for Cornish miners. The half-moon shape is essential and it is a said that a genuine Cornish pasty will not break if accidentally dropped down a mineshaft.

In Scotland the **Scotch pie** has been a favourite for many years. A double-crust pie containing minced mutton, the Scotch pie is the half-time hot snack of choice at football matches north of the border. The finest examples of this pie can be tasted each year at the World Scotch Pie Championships in the Fife town of Dunfermline. North of Fife is the county of Angus, home of a minced meat and onion turnover called a **bridie**. This is a speciality of the town of Forfar and its name may be a shortening of 'bride's pie', a former wedding-day treat in those parts.

The origin of the phrase 'eating humble pie' is not entirely abstract and comes from a pie made from the entrails or 'umbles' of a deer. A genuinely humble pie was a wartime standby called the **Woolton pie**. Named after the 1st Earl of Woolton, who was Britain's Minister of Food in World War II, the pie was made from leftover vegetables. Its lack of meat – due to wartime shortages – meant that it was not an especially welcome item on 1940s menu and it was quickly retired when rationing ended.

A savoury with a far more exalted place in Britain's pantheon of pies is that delicious combination of hot-water pastry, uncured chopped pork, jelly, and a dash of spice: the **pork pie**. Strongly associated with the town of Melton Mowbray in Leicestershire, the pork pie is served cold and is a feature of a **ploughman's lunch** or might be eaten on its own. The mini or 'cocktail' pork pie is a recent and welcome addition to cold buffets.

Another welcome sight is the **shepherd's pie**. This pie, traditionally made from leftover minced mutton, also contains onions in a thick gravy and is topped with a layer of mashed potatoes. The pie is then baked until the mash is brown. For the shepherd's pie the clue is in the name: it contains mutton, and should not under any circumstances be confused with the **cottage pie**, a similar savoury made from minced beef.

Last but not least is **toad-in-the-hole**, a baked batter pudding containing sausages. The concept dates back to Roman times and more recent incarnations might have involved pigeon. Sausage, however, is the preferred 'toad' nowadays and this dish is a firm dinner-time favourite of schoolchildren.

THE PROOF OF
THE PUDDING

The word 'pudding' dates to medieval times but the first ones
that history records were savoury rather than sweet, consisting of
fillings put into a casing and then boiled like a sausage. First we
will briefly look at Britain's savoury puddings and then, for afters,
we'll work our way through the better known members of the
sweet variety.

The **black pudding** and the **haggis** (Scotland's 'great chieftain
o' the puddin'-race') have already been described in this book,
so we shall consider two savoury puddings that are many people's
idea of Sunday-lunch heaven. The **Yorkshire pudding** is made
from a batter of milk, eggs, and flour baked in beef dripping
until crisp, puffy, and golden brown. It deflates like a soufflé
when removed from the oven so should be served immediately
with its classic accompaniment, roast beef. At the opposite end of
England is Sussex, which is credited as the home of the **steak and
kidney pudding**, a combination of suet-crust pastry filled with
stewing beef, kidney, and gravy. It was first noted in a recipe by
the great Victorian cookery writer, Mrs Beeton.

For most of us, however, the word 'pudding' conjures up
something sweet – one of those stick-to-your-ribs desserts served
with custard and associated with Sunday lunch, school dinners,
and a past era when winters were colder and appetites heartier.

The family of steamed **suet puddings**, made from flour, suet,
sugar, and various combinations of dried fruit, has some notable
members. **Plum duff** (from an old northern pronunciation of
'dough') does not necessarily contain dried plums (prunes) and
the ingredients depend on the cook. This type of pudding was
once sold as a street food, and its sellers were known as 'plum-
duffers'. Similarly constituted is the **Christmas pudding** which
gets its darker hue from black treacle and longer cooking.
The Christmas pudding is traditionally steamed in a cloth,

topped with a sprig of holly, and then brought to the table in darkness where it is doused in brandy and set alight. Custard or brandy butter is the usual accompaniment and good luck comes to whoever finds the silver coin – formerly a sixpence – hidden in the pudding.

From Scotland comes another dark and heavy dessert, the **clootie dumpling**. A similar coin-hiding ritual is associated with this suet pudding, whose name comes from the *cloot* (cloth) in which it is steamed. Our final member of the suet clan is **spotted dick**, which means simply 'speckled pudding' and not anything coarse (despite obvious misunderstandings).

The term 'roly-poly' has a long history. It started off meaning 'a rascal', and then it was used to describe various ball games, before becoming an irreverent word for peas, and finally, in Victorian times, a pudding. **Jam roly-poly** consists of suet crust which is spread with jam and then rolled up and steamed. Sometimes nicknamed 'dead man's arm', it is a nursery favourite.

The **rice pudding** dates back hundreds of years. Made from pudding rice, milk, sugar, and a sprinkling of spices, it is best baked in the oven, where it develops a golden-brown skin. Some say this skin is the best feature of the dish, although it has become part of an insult where a person's strength is impugned thus: 'You couldn't knock the skin off a rice pudding!'

Finally we come to an ancient English pudding, the **syllabub**. A Tudor creation, it involves curdling cream by mixing it with wine or cider, and there is a thick version for eating and a thin version for drinking. The name is a mystery, although the current spelling is perhaps due to the influence of the word 'syllable'.

A PIECE OF CAKE!

The British love a nice piece of cake, especially with their morning coffee or at the traditional tea time of four o'clock. In this section we look at some of the different cakes that you might find as you travel around around the British Isles.

Many of the cakes you will find in Britain's bakeries and teashops started out as local delicacies and bear the name of the town or city in which they were originally baked – although they may now be much more widely available. The **Bakewell tart**, for example, is named after the town of Bakewell in Derbyshire. This cake is an uncovered tart with a pastry base and a layer of jam. In between the pastry and jam is a layer of almond-flavoured sponge cake.

From the Scottish city of Dundee comes the **Dundee cake**. This rich fruit cakes is traditionally decorated with almonds. It was first marketed in the nineteenth century, but was based on a much older recipe.

The **Banbury cake** consists of a pastry base filled with currants, raisins, candied peel, and sugar, with a crisscross pattern on the top. It comes from the town of Banbury in Oxfordshire, and the crisscross pattern may allude to the famous Banbury Cross which is immortalized in a children's rhyme.

The **Eccles cake** is a similar currant-filled pastry that takes its name from the town of Eccles in Lancashire – once a village but now a part of Manchester. The currants in the filling have been compared rather unkindly to dead insects in appearance, leading to the cake's nickname of 'squashed fly cake' or even 'fly cemetery'.

One pastry that bucks the convention of naming cakes after the place where they were originally created is the **Sally Lunn**, a flat round cake made from a sweet yeast dough. This is said to be named after an eighteenth-century English baker who invented it in Bath in Somerset. In other versions of the story, Sally Lunn was a girl who sold the cakes in the town rather than the person who baked them.

Other names reflect a cake's characteristic ingredients rather than its place of origin. The **lardy cake**, for example, is a rich, sweet cake which features lard as a major ingredient (along with bread dough, sugar, and dried fruit). Similarly, **tipsy cake** is so called because the sponge cake that forms its base is soaked with white wine or sherry before being decorated with almonds and crystallized fruit.

The origins of the **simnel cake** are not so transparent. This is a fruit cake containing a layer of marzipan. It is often coloured with saffron and has an additional layer of marzipan on the top. The name of the cake comes from an Old French word, and can be traced ultimately to the Latin *simila*, meaning 'fine flour'. It is traditionally eaten at Lent or Easter.

On the other hand, a **teacake** doesn't include tea in its recipe. Rather, this flat cake made with raisins is considered a perfect accompaniment to afternoon tea, especially when it is toasted and buttered.

> The largest cake ever baked in Britain stood at a height of nine feet and three inches. It was created in 2009 by Michael Burns of Uddingston, Lanarkshire. Mr Burns was a baker by profession, and worked at the town's famous biscuit factory. He created the record-breaking fifteen-tier cake to mark the occasion of his own marriage. When it was finished, the cake was so large that a forklift truck was required to transport it to the wedding reception.

LIFE IS SWEET!

The term 'sweet tooth' is first noted in English in the fourteenth century, but we had to wait a further five hundred years for the kind of confectionery we know today – chocolate bars, boiled sweets, and soft chews. Join us in the tuck shop as we find out how the Victorians invented some of our favourite treats.

Britain was the first nation to become industrialized and in 1851 some of the miracles of the Industrial Revolution were shown at the Great Exhibition in the Crystal Palace. The latest mechanical marvels were showcased but there was also a display of **boiled sweets**. Until then sweets had been hand-made, but factories could now churn them out cheaply and the new railway network could distribute them widely. Confectionery became big business and 'sweet stall', 'sweet shop', and 'sweet maker' all made their appearance in the language.

Chocolate also became big business. There was snobbishness towards 'trade' as Establishment families (chiefly members of the Anglican Church) tended to go into the law, the universities, and the military. Protestant nonconformists such as the Quakers were shut out from the professions (and as pacifists avoided the army), and many gravitated towards confectionery. The Cadburys of Birmingham, the Frys of Bristol, and the Rowntrees and Terrys of York were Quaker families who made money from confectionery but are also remembered as campaigners for social justice. The Cadbury brothers, for example, created Bourneville village, a large site where workers lived in affordable housing in pleasant surroundings with facilities for sport and recreation.

The Cadburys were members of the temperance movement and provided workers with tea and chocolate to lure them away from alcohol. Charles Maynard was also teetotal, and he took a great deal of persuading by his namesake son in 1909 to make a product called **wine gums**. The father relented and the fruit-flavoured but non-alcoholic chews have been in sweet shops ever since.

Sweets of a similar vintage are **liquorice allsorts**, whose creation is down to accident rather than design. In 1899 an employee at the firm of Bassett's dropped samples of sweets when showing them to a wholesaler, but the resulting assortment pleased the buyer so much he wanted to buy the batch in that form. This '**pick-and-mix**' attitude to confectionery lasts to this day and there was great sadness in 2008 when Woolworth's, a regular destination for sweet-loving children, went out of business.

Liquorice allsorts were not the first British sweets to contain liquorice. A Yorkshire legend claims that a schoolmaster from Pontefract, on a day out to the east coast, discovered liquorice sticks washed up on the shore from a shipwrecked galleon of the Spanish Armada. He found these useful for thrashing schoolboys but the pupils preferred to eat them. This unlikely creation myth is behind the **Pontefract cake**, a flat, round disc of liquorice made in the Yorkshire town which celebrates liquorice by holding an annual festival in its honour.

Celebrations also took place in 1918 following the end of the First World War, and Bassett's marked the Armistice by creating a product called 'Peace Babies'. Production ceased during the next conflict due to rationing, but these soft sweets were re-introduced in 1953 and renamed **Jelly Babies**. In an interview a young George Harrison stated that he liked Jelly Babies. Fans then started to throw the soft sweets at the Beatles at concerts. This was fine in Britain, but not in America, where only harder 'jelly beans' were available. Harrison was hit by such a sweet, a stinging experience that may have hastened the Fab Four's decision to retire from performing live.

TAKING THE BISCUIT

The word 'biscuit', like much of the vocabulary of food, comes from French and means 'twice-cooked'. The origins of the biscuit may have a French connection, but the tradition of having a sit-down with a biscuit and a nice cup of tea couldn't be more British. Here we look at some of the more celebrated biscuits to come from these islands.

❖ The origin of the **Abernethy biscuit** has nothing to do with the Perthshire town of that name. Instead, these hard biscuits were invented by a British physician, Dr John Abernethy (1764–1831), who was interested in all matters dietary. The original Abernethy was a ship's biscuit to which was added sugar (for energy) and caraway seeds (which were thought to improve digestion).

❖ The **Bath Oliver** is a hard, unsweetened cracker also invented by a medical man, Dr William Oliver (1695–1764) of Bath. He was the founder of a hospital in that city, and in his will left the recipe for the biscuit to his coachman, Atkins, who set up a biscuit business and became a wealthy man.

❖ The Bath Oliver and the Abernethy are both based on the original hard, dry biscuit: the **ship's biscuit**. Baked hard with a minimum of water, these were a feature of a sailor's diet on long maritime voyages from the sixteenth century until the First World War. Indeed, in *As You Like It* Shakespeare described something 'As drie as the remainder bisket After a voyage'. Ship's biscuits were preserved in wooden barrels and often infested with weevils, a very unwelcome source of protein in the naval diet.

❖ The **oatcake**, like porridge, has long been a part of the Scottish diet, and Samuel Johnson famously defined oats as 'a grain that is fed to horses in England and to people in Scotland'. The English clergyman and wit Sydney

Smith, although a co-founder of the *Edinburgh Review*, commented mischievously on the diet and religious affiliations north of the border by stating that Scotland was a 'land of Calvin, oatcakes, and sulphur'.

❖ Also strongly associated with Scotland is that sweet and butter-rich concoction, **shortbread**. Although it is eaten all year round, shortbread is considered an important feature of traditional Scottish Christmas and New Year festivities. It usually comes in flat oblong biscuits or triangular 'petticoat tails'.

❖ The **garibaldi** is a rectangular biscuit with two layers of soft sweet biscuit separated by a layer of minced currants. It gets his name from Giuseppe Garibaldi, a nationalist whose military campaigns led to Italian unification in the nineteenth century. He visited Britain and was accorded the honour of having a biscuit named after him. The garibaldi, due to its appearance, is sometimes called the 'squashed-fly biscuit'.

❖ The **ginger nut**, known originally as the 'gingerbread nut', was first noted in the eighteenth century. The 'nut' part of the name leads us to assume that they were smaller than the biscuits we know today.

The British value biscuits not just for their taste but also for their 'dunkability' – the ability to stay relatively solid when dipped into hot tea. The practice of dunking biscuits was the subject of a memorable advertising slogan of the 1970s: 'a drink's too wet without one'. It was also the subject of research by an English physicist, Dr Len Fisher, whose dunking experiments resulted in the formulation of an equation which won him an Ig Nobel Prize, an award that gently satirizes dubious contributions to science.

SAY CHEESE!

Some of the world's favourite cheeses come from these shores. Here we look at the best-known British varieties and examine the recent revival of traditional cheese-making techniques.

The American writer Clifton Fadiman described cheese as 'milk's leap toward immortality'. Many modern connoisseurs of cheese would agree with this assessment, although until relatively recently cheese in Britain was considered a humble, albeit a very tasty, food. Jonathan Swift referred to bread and cheese as 'bachelor's fare', but cheese is certainly the only thing that makes cauliflower interesting to eat and is often the best part of that ubiquitous pub staple the **ploughman's lunch**.

Until the Industrial Revolution, cheese in Britain was made in small batches by artisans. Time was allowed for the cheese to mature, and many towns and counties were famed for cheeses unique to their own area. Industrialization mechanized the processes and in the lengthy rationing era during and after the Second World War many traditional cheese-makers went out of business. Unpasteurized cheeses were also frowned upon and cheese in Britain for a time was generally processed, artificially coloured, and bland.

Fortunately, a renaissance has taken place in recent decades. Old techniques have been revived, artisan cheese-makers are lauded, and cheesemongers are flourishing once again. There is now much more to cheese than **Welsh rarebit** (fine dish though it is), and Britain now vies with France as Europe's cheese capital. Charles de Gaulle said that France is 'ungovernable' because it is home to '246 different types of cheese'. Britain must be heading towards that figure as it regains pride in its cheeses and seeks to get them recognized as regional specialities through acquiring Protected Geographical Status.

❖ **Cheddar** is Britain's best-known hard cheese and takes its name from a village in Somerset in south-west England where production of the cheese first began before the end of the sixteenth century. Cheeses from all around the world are called 'cheddar', but the name now refers to the pressing process of 'cheddaring' that gives the cheese its smooth texture.

❖ **Stilton** is England's most celebrated blue cheese. Named in the eighteenth century after the village of Stilton in Huntingdonshire where it was first sold, the cheese can only legally be called Stilton if it is made in Leicestershire, Nottinghamshire, or Derbyshire. This means, rather confusingly, that Stilton from Stilton cannot be called Stilton.

❖ A town in Wales gives its name to our next cheese, **Caerphilly**. A tangy cows'-milk cheese, Caerphilly was once the lunch-time favourite of Welsh miners.

❖ The valley of **Wensleydale** is home to a crumbly cheese that is the pride of Yorkshire. It is also the favourite cheese of the animated duo Wallace & Gromit whose appreciation of Wensleydale has resulted in a recent increase in sales.

❖ From England's south-west come two favourites, **Single** and **Double Gloucester**, both of which are used in Gloucestershire's contribution to extreme sports: **cheese rolling**.

❖ From the same county comes **Stinking Bishop**, a soft cheese entirely inappropriate for pursuing down steep hills. Its rind is washed in perry (pear cider) made from Stinking Bishop pears, a variety named posthumously after a Mr Bishop who apparently had a bit of a temper.

❖ Our final cheese is a recent concoction from Cornwall and is called **Yarg**. This is not an old Cornish word but simply the name 'Gray' (the surname of the couple who created the cheese) spelt backwards.

AS BRITISH AS FISH
AND CHIPS

A French writer once observed that 'the best English cooking is, of course, simply French cooking'. This was just after the Second World War, when the classiest British restaurants served French food, had menus in French, and even translated the names of British dishes into French to give them a veneer of sophistication. British cookery has always been quick to adopt and then adapt foreign dishes. Here we examine the cuisines that have most influenced British cooking.

Some of the foods we think of as British have foreign origins. Without Columbus's voyages to the Americas there would be no **potatoes** for the chips in **fish and chips**, no **turkey** for **Christmas dinner**, and no **chocolate** for digestive biscuits.

The **tomato** was once an exotic import and originally kept as an ornamental plant as it was thought to be poisonous. In the seventeenth century **pepper** and **tea** were so expensive that the former was used as currency while the latter had to be kept in locked chests. The **pineapple** caused a huge stir when it appeared in Britain. Only the rich could afford to eat them and the fruit even became a decorative motif on the houses of some wealthy eccentrics.

The exotic quality of these imports has long since worn off. In any British roadside cafe tomatoes will appear in ketchup form, pepper will be a humble condiment alongside the salt, tea will be the cheapest thing on the menu, and pineapples will be served in chunks from a tin.

One cuisine that typifies the transition from exotic to everyday is **Indian**. The 'Jewel in the Crown' of Britain's former empire, India was a country that British soldiers, traders, and administrators couldn't quite get out of their system, and many wanted a taste of India when they returned home. In her 1747 cookbook Hannah Glasse featured a recipe for 'currey' and a century later Mrs Beeton noted that curry powder could be obtained from 'any respectable shop'. Curry powder, of course, is a key ingredient in those two classic Anglo-Indian dishes **kedgeree** and **Coronation chicken** (the latter created to celebrate Elizabeth II's coronation in 1953).

The end of the Second World War heralded the end of empire, but not Britain's interest in Indian food. Several waves of immigration soon gave every town an Indian restaurant and the cuisine was co-opted to suit British tastes. The '**boil-in-the-bag**' curry was a staple in the 1970s and by the turn of the twenty-first century Britain's Foreign Secretary Robin Cook noted that **chicken tikka massala** (originally a dry dish, but given a tomato sauce on arrival in Britain) was a 'true British national dish'.

Italian food has exerted an even longer influence on British cuisine. During the Great Fire of London in 1666, diarist Samuel Pepys buried his valuable **Parmesan** cheeses, and in the following century **macaroni cheese** was first noted in a British cookbook. Despite this, pasta was still a mystery to many Britons, and in the 1950s and a BBC programme on April Fools' Day tricked viewers into believing that spaghetti was grown on trees in Italy. It soon became commonplace. **Spaghetti bolognaise** has become the midweek staple **spag bol** and tinned **alphabet spaghetti** is a favourite with children. **Pizza** has been similarly anglified. The full English breakfast pizza is an unlikely start to the day, while in Glasgow pizza (like every other food) can be deep-fried.

New imported dishes will eventually go through the same process. From exotic speciality, to pub classic, to midweek favourite, to sandwich filling, and then to the final stage of acceptance: becoming a flavour of crisps.

HERE FOR THE BEER

The French philosopher Voltaire commented that the British 'are like their own beer: froth on top, dregs at the bottom, the middle excellent'. Here we don our beer goggles and look at the high points, and the low, in the history of beer in Britain.

Like other northern lands Britain is a beer-drinking country. The Romans imported wine to Britain which was drunk by the Romanized population, but once the colonists left **ale** took over once more. From Anglo-Saxon times until the late Middle Ages ale was drunk by most of the population, adults and children, as the purity of drinking water could not be relied on. In the fifteenth century English brewers followed their Flemish counterparts and started adding **hops** to ale to make beer. The hops added flavour and acted as a preservative and soon hops were planted in England, particularly in Kent, the 'garden of England'.

As small breweries expanded into large commercial operations, brewing styles changed. **Porter** and **stout**, both dark beers, were the most popular types in the eighteenth century, but lighter-coloured bitter beers such as **pale ale** came into vogue in the nineteenth century. Brewing flourished as legislation was enacted against 'mother's ruin' – gin.

Mass production and the merger of small breweries into large 'megabreweries' after the second war led to a decline in traditional beers. **Keg beer** – filtered, pasteurized and served from metal containers rather than wooden barrels – was bland but became widespread, along with lager. Some drinkers objected and the **Campaign for Real Ale** (CAMRA) was born. Independent breweries re-emerged to satisfy a desire for variety and flavour. Brewing underwent a renaissance and now **craft beers** brewed in **microbreweries** compete successfully against the multinationals.

Beer terminology differs from country to country, even within the UK. Here is an explanation of British beer types:

- **Bitter** describes usually light-coloured beers with a high content of hops. Similar beers include **pale ale** and **India Pale Ale**, supposedly called because of the increased levels of hops needed to preserve the beer on the voyage to the Subcontinent.

- **Brown ales** are darker and sweeter than pale ales and the most famous of all hails from Newcastle. **Mild** is similarly coloured but has a low alcohol content.

- **Porter** is one of the oldest types of beer, its biscuit and coffee flavours coming from the use of roasted malts. The name derives from its association with the porters who drank it in the eighteenth century. A similar beer is **stout**, also black, which was commonly brewed in Britain in Victorian times but which has since became synonymous with Ireland.

- **Barley wine**, despite the name, has nothing to do with grapes. It is a strong ale whose name was inspired by a drink made by the ancient Greeks.

- Scottish beers are often classified according to the number of shillings (an old British coin) formerly payable on a barrel. The two most popular beers served in Scottish pubs are **70 shilling** (also called **heavy**) and the stronger **80 shilling** (also called **export**). Shillings are no longer used as money but the beer names stuck.

Real ales are traditionally given names that invoke a rural heritage, such as 'Old Speckled Hen'. Other breweries go in for wordplay ('Cereal Killer', anyone?), while many have connotations of smut ('Old Leg-Over', for example). Britain's military history is plundered ('Lancaster Bomber', 'Nelson's Revenge'). Last but not least, drunkenness is a rich seam, with 'Sozzled Swine', 'Carry Me Home', and 'Tipsy Trotter' to name but three. Cheers!

WHISKY GALORE!

'One whisky is all right; two is too much; three is too few.'
This Highland proverb probably rings true with most whisky
drinkers, and here we will look into the history of **whisky**, its place
in Scottish culture, and explain some of the terms you might hear
in a Scottish pub.

Like Christianity, strong drink is thought to have arrived in
Scotland courtesy of Irish missionaries. In Ireland they spell it
'whiskey' with an 'e', but both spellings have the same Gaelic
origin: *uisge beatha* meaning 'the water of life'.

For much of whisky's history its distillers fought a battle
against taxes and licensing laws. Illicit stills sprang up, especially
in the remote Highlands far away from snooping excise men.
Even excise men could see that the laws were punitive and one of
their number, a certain Robert Burns, wrote a poem of complaint
which had the memorable line 'Freedom and whisky gang
thegither!'

Things improved in the nineteenth century. The Excise Act
of 1823 cut drastically the excise paid on the drink and royal
patronage helped whisky improve its reputation. The novelist
Sir Walter Scott toasted the visiting monarch William IV with
whisky, and Queen Victoria enjoyed a dram at her Balmoral
retreat in Deeside so much that she gave several distilleries
Royal Warrants.

In the 1880s an outbreak of phylloxera in France devastated
the wine and brandy trades. What was bad for brandy was good
for whisky and the Scottish spirit enjoyed a boom period.

Whisky is the national drink in Scotland. Boats are launched,
babies christened, and toasts made with whisky rather than
champagne, and glasses of the spirit are raised at the two most
important annual celebrations of all things Scottish, **Burns Night**
(25 January) and **Hogmanay** (New Year's Eve).

Before we continue, some of the language of whisky needs to
be explained. Whisky is drunk in **drams** (an amount dependent

on the generosity of the pourer), and in pubs you might hear a whisky referred to as a **wee goldie**. Some drinkers might call whisky **the cratur** (a Scots rendering of 'creature') and others will order a **hauf and a hauf** (a whisky and a half pint of beer).

The kind of unpretentious whisky reserved for dilution with lemonade is a **blended whisky**, which is a mix of malt and grain whiskies from a number of distilleries. The more upmarket whiskies are called **single malts**, which are entirely comprised of a single distillery's whisky made from a mash using one particular malted grain.

Mixing a single malt with anything other than a small dash of water will result in a weary sigh from a Scottish drinking companion as single malts are the Rolls Royces of the whisky world and, generally, the older the malt the more expensive the whisky. Lengthy storage in wooden barrels, perhaps previously used to store bourbon or sherry, will impart numerous flavours to whisky and send connoisseurs into rhapsodies.

Whisky in Scotland, like wine in France, is categorized by region. An imaginary line between Dundee in the east and Greenock in the west marks the boundary between **Highland** and **Lowland**, although **Speyside** (an area roughly from Aberdeen to Inverness) is a Highland region unto itself. The Hebridean island of **Islay** is noted for pungent, peaty whiskies, while nearby **Campbeltown** on the Mull of Kintyre used to have thirty-two distilleries. The **Island** region encompasses Arran in the southwest, the Hebrides (except Islay), and Orkney to the north.

Some pubs will stock whiskies from every region, which might prompt you to repeat Samuel Johnson's words: 'Come, let me know what it is that makes a Scotchman happy!'

THE
COUNTRYSIDE

THE GREAT
OUTDOORS

At the time of the Norman Conquest in 1066, only around five per cent of the British people lived in towns. Britain was an agricultural nation, and this was reflected in its language, its proverbs, and its traditions. The Industrial Revolution of the eighteenth century brought about a fundamental change in the structure of our society: the British now became predominantly an urban race, and for many the countryside was known only as the scene of holidays and recreation. Yet in spite of this shift to the towns we still remember much of the wisdom of our rural ancestors. We still say 'Red sky at night, shepherd's delight' and 'Never cast a clout till may is out', even though there are few shepherds left to take pleasure from a rosy sunset and few of us have a maytree handy so that we can check when to don our summer clothes.

As our cities have spread out into the countryside, the forests and meadows have correspondingly shrunk, but Britain is still blessed with some spectacular scenery. Moreover, there is a thriving movement that aims to conserve as much of it as possible. Some of the finest areas of countryside have been designated as national parks so that they can be protected from further development. There are 15 such parks at present, including Dartmoor, the New Forest, and the Lake District in England, Snowdonia and the Brecon Beacons in Wales, and Loch Lomond and the Trossachs, which forms a single national park in Scotland. Other sites are protected as 'areas of outstanding natural beauty' (AONBs), while those that preserve rare flora, fauna, or rock formations may be designated as 'sites of special scientific interest' (SSSIs). There are also other categories of protected area, including National Nature Reserves, Ramsar Sites (protected wetlands), and Special Protection Areas (for wild birds).

So with all of this countryside to explore, we now head for the great outdoors and pay tribute to England's green and pleasant land, to the bonny banks of Loch Lomond, to the green valleys of Wales, and to the beauty of the Emerald Isle where the Mountains of Mourne come down to the sea.

Our first stop is at the farm gate, where we ponder the history of some of the agricultural breeds that are peculiar to the British Isles, before we consider the controversial country pursuit of fox-hunting and learn some of the language of the chase. We then don our binoculars to view some of the country's native birds, relishing the delightful dialect names that have been attached to these creatures, and noting how they have been a source of inspiration to the nation's creative artists.

Moving from the animal kingdom to the plant kingdom, we then consider the trees that grace the nation's orchards, woods, and forests and the flowers that can be found in its hedgerows, fields, and meadows. Some of these have names that take us back to the days when people lived hand in hand with nature and the behaviour of plants gave us essential information about the time and the weather. Moreover, plants have always had a strong symbolic importance, and we shall explore some of the intriguing stories and legends that are associated with them.

At the end of our trip to the countryside, we shall engage in that most British of all pastimes and have a natter about the weather. It soon becomes clear that the British have lots of different words for fogs, mists, and rains, but seemingly fewer words to describe sunshine!

DOWN ON THE FARM

Britain's temperate maritime climate means that winters are generally mild, summers not too hot, and there is no shortage of rain, particularly in the west. This means that we have near perfect conditions for livestock farming. So let us don our wellies and look at some of the breeds of animal that have originated in these islands, many of which have been exported around the world.

Looking at cattle first, we start in Scotland with a breed famous for the quality of its meat: the **Aberdeen Angus**. Hugh Watson of Angus is credited with being this hornless breed's founder, and most members of the breed can be traced to two of his cattle, a bull called Old Jock and a cow named Old Granny. Old Granny was a venerable beast, calving twenty-nine times and living to the age of thirty-five when she met a tragic end during a lightning storm.

Staying north of the border we find a breed that symbolizes Scotland: the **Highland cattle**. Having reddish-brown shaggy hair and long, curved widely spaced horns, the Highland cow is a very hardy breed able to browse for food on mountainous terrain. It is a popular subject for visiting painters and photographers, and visitors to the Burrell Collection, an art gallery in Glasgow, can see a small prize-winning herd of the beasts in its home in Pollok Park.

At the opposite end of the country, nearer the French coastline than the English, are the Channel Islands, two of which give their name to a famous breed of dairy cattle. The **Guernsey** is a hardy but docile cow, fawn-coloured with white markings. Its milk has a golden tinge and is rich in vitamin A. To the south is **Jersey** whose cattle are equally docile but more graceful. Jersey milk has a slightly higher buttermilk content than that of the Guernsey, and both creamy milks are known as 'breakfast milk' on the British mainland, where they are favoured for making puddings.

Britain is also home to some distinctive breeds of horse, from the tiny **Shetland pony** to some mighty draught horses. The **Clydesdale**, named after the Clyde valley where the breed originated, is a high-standing and quick-stepping horse noted for its shaggy legs and good disposition. Clydesdales were exported to America, where a noted team pulls carts for the Budweiser brewery.

A similar breed, but slightly larger, is the **shire horse**, a majestic English animal that was the main source of pulling power on farms before mechanization. Much admired, shire horses continue to perform ceremonial cart-pulling duties for a number of traditional English brewers.

From East Anglia is the **Suffolk Punch**, a chestnut horse noted for its former role in pulling non-motorized transport and also artillery pieces in a number of wars. The horse also appears on the crest of Suffolk's main football team, Ipswich Town, where it can be seen trapping a ball under its hoof.

Last, but not least, are two famous breeds of pig. The large dark patches on the skin of the **Gloucester Old Spot**, according to local folklore, are bruises caused by falling fruit. The breed was immortalized in 1834 by the artist John Miles in a painting of one particularly prodigious porker, said to be the largest pig ever bred in Britain.

From Staffordshire is the **Tamworth**, a hardy pig that resulted from the interbreeding of local swine with a herd from Ireland. Its most celebrated members are the 'Tamworth Two', a brother and sister who escaped the slaughterhouse and went on the run in 1998. When finally recaptured the public wanted them saved and the escapees, now named Butch and Sundance, finished their days contented, like pigs in clover, at an animal sanctuary in Kent.

TALLY-HO!

Hunting is either a great British tradition or, in the words of the eighteenth-century poet William Cowper, a 'detested sport that owes its pleasure to another's pain'. The best known British field sport (or blood sport if you prefer) is undoubtedly **fox-hunting**. It is also the most controversial and has been the subject of much heated debate and attempts to ban it outright.

Fox-hunting as a means of pest control has been a feature of country life for hundreds of years but it wasn't until the nineteenth century that 'riding to hounds' came to be regarded as the chief winter pastime of the landed gentry. Like many country pursuits it has a season (from November to April) and a set of traditions that can best be explained by delving into the vocabulary of the sport.

Fox-hunting is where huntsmen and huntswomen on horseback pursue a fox accompanied by a pack of hounds who hunt their quarry by following its scent. The **master of foxhounds** (sometimes shortened to MFH) is in charge of each hunt and is responsible for maintaining the foxhounds and the associated staff and equipment. The MFH is assisted by **whippers-in** who control the hounds during the hunt. The dogs track the fox's scent then flush it out of its lair or 'earth' and the hunt by the dogs begins, with the mounted followers – **the field** – in close pursuit.

The traditional clothes of the huntsmen are scarlet jackets, called **pinks**, and white riding breeches. Such apparel makes a hunt hard to miss and the sound of a huntsman blasting a call on his hunting horn will also alert the unwary rambler or birdwatcher. The horn's call is not the only noise associated with a foxhunt. To encourage the hounds the huntsmen will shout **hoicks** and when the fox is spotted cries of **view halloo** and **tally-ho** might be heard.

Despite, or perhaps because of, fox-hunting's long associations with Britain's aristocracy and royalty there has always been opposition to it and other forms of hunting. In the Victorian era

the dramatist WS Gilbert (of opera-writing duo Gilbert and
Sullivan) noted of deer-stalking that it 'would be a very fine sport
if only the deer had guns', while slightly later Oscar Wilde
memorably described fox-hunting as 'the unspeakable in full
pursuit of the uneatable'.

Such eloquent attacks on the sport perhaps inspired future
generations of opponents. The **League Against Cruel Sports** was
formed in 1924 and by 1949 a bill was put forward in parliament
seeking to ban fox-hunting.

The bill failed but opposition gathered pace. Hunt saboteurs
(known informally as **sabs**) were prepared to take direct and
often violent action against hunts, while some politicians (usually
– but not always – urban and left-wing) attempted again to ban the
sport. This succeeded and hunting with dogs is now illegal on the
British mainland.

Followers of country pursuits have not given up on fox-hunting
and the **Countryside Alliance** and other members of rural Britain's
green-welly brigade are intent on overturning the ban. For them
fox-hunting is not only necessary to keep the fox population in
check but a tradition that binds many rural populations together.
They note that Nazi Germany was the first country to ban fox-
hunting and describe the new legislation 'as illiberal as the laws
that once deprived Jews and Catholics of political rights'. These
words were penned by conservative philosopher Roger Scruton,
a man noted for trying to popularize the eating of fox meat. His
efforts in this direction have failed but attempts to overturn the
ban on fox-hunting might be more successful.

OUR FEATHERED FRIENDS

The British are a nation of bird-lovers. Our gardens are full of bird-feeders, bird-baths, and nesting boxes. **Bird-watchers** are to be found in every habitat and '**twitchers**' (competitive bird-watchers) will head off to the opposite end of the country at a moment's notice to catch sight of a rare species. Here we take a bird's-eye view of Britain, looking at the folklore that surrounds its birds, the art they have inspired, and some of the unusual local names we have for them.

In Europe the **robin** is not inclined to associate with people, but on these shores it is popular with anyone with a garden because of its friendly nature and appetite for insect pests. It has long been associated with Christianity, for example, in the proverb 'The robin redbreast and the wren are God Almighty's cock and hen'. Legend has it that the robin got its red breast when it injured itself plucking a thorn from Christ's crown of thorns. There is also an old myth that if a robin found someone lying dead it would cover their face with leaves or flowers.

It is considered bad luck to harm a robin or its eggs. A similar belief surrounds the nest of a **martin**: having one on your house is good luck but destroying it will bring bad luck, such as your cows giving bloody milk.

A more pleasant tradition concerns the **cuckoo**. In some English counties the sound of the first cuckoo of spring prompted workers to down tools, claim the day as a holiday, and drink beer out of doors to toast the bird in a tradition called '**wetting the cuckoo**'.

A more recent tradition involves readers of *The Times* competing to get a letter published where they claim to have heard the first cuckoo of the year, and perhaps this inspired composer Frederick Delius to pen his famous tone poem 'On Hearing the First Cuckoo of Spring'. His fellow composer,

Ralph Vaughan Williams, was inspired by a **skylark** and in 'The Lark Ascending' the violin mimics the soaring flight and vocals of that bird.

Poets in these islands, from John Milton to Ted Hughes, have also been inspired by birds. Perhaps the best-loved poem on an avian theme is John Keats' 'Ode to a Nightingale' where the poet is put into a reverie by a **nightingale** that 'singest of summer in full-throated ease'.

Keats might have been familiar with some of the more poetic names our ancestors gave to birds. Here is a selection of some taken from a dictionary of British folk names published in 1912:

Bessy Brantail	a Shropshire name for the redstart
Big Mavis	an East Lothian name for the mistle thrush
bog jumper	the bittern
Charlie Muftie	a Scots name for the whitethroat
Mizzly Dick	a Northumberland name for the mistle thrush
Molly Washdish	a Somerset name for the pied wagtail
Peepy Lennart	a Holy Island name for the twite
sit-ye-down	the great titmouse
swing-devil	a Northumberland name for the swift
toad snatcher	a Yorkshire name for the reed bunting
watery pleeps	an Orkney name for the sandpiper
yaffle	the green woodpecker

HEARTS OF OAK

There are many famous trees, woods, and forests in the British Isles. Let us take a walk in the woods as we look at the role trees have played in some of the myths, legends, and fascinating chapters in our history.

The British Isles used to be covered in forests. Ancient man then discovered how useful wood is and the felling of trees for fuel and as a building material started in earnest, but some forests were protected, usually as hunting grounds for royals and aristocrats. Hampshire's **New Forest** was where William the Conqueror relaxed but it wasn't a happy hunting ground for his son, William II, who was mortally wounded by an arrow that glanced off an oak tree.

The **oak**, the 'Monarch of the Forest', is synonymous with England. Celtic Druids in ancient times venerated the oak, perhaps for its longevity. More modern Britons favoured the tree for its hard, durable wood, perfect for constructing ships in the age of sail where around 3,500 mature oaks were required to build a battleship. It was said that both Britain's ships and its sailors had a '**heart of oak**', a sentiment summed up in an eighteenth-century patriotic song of that name.

Oaks are also good for hiding in, and Charles II did just that after a defeat at the Battle of Worcester in 1651. He then fled England but returned in triumph after a short period of rule under Oliver Cromwell. The original **Royal Oak**, in Boscobel Wood, is no longer there but a descendant supposedly grows in its place.

The legendary Robin Hood is also said to have both hidden in an oak in **Sherwood Forest** and married Maid Marian under its boughs. This tree was originally known as the Queen Oak but got its current name, the **Major Oak**, after an eighteenth-century military man, Major Hayman Rooke. The tree was recently cloned so that a replica can be grown when the original dies.

Also in Nottinghamshire was the **Parliament Oak**. This tree was where Edward I held an impromptu parliament when he heard that the Welsh were rebelling under Llywelyn ap Gruffydd. The Welsh were defeated – as they had been earlier at Nevern Castle, the site of a mysterious tree called the **Bleeding Yew**, which exudes a red liquid from its trunk. Legend holds that the tree will bleed until a Welshman holds the ruined Nevern Castle again, although some say that the liquid is the blood of those buried in the nearby graveyard of St Brynach.

Across the Irish Sea we consider two ancient legends, one concerning a sacred tree planted by the Druids. A girl was tempted by the tree's fruit but was drowned by a fountain of water which erupted from the tree and formed the River Shannon. To the north is the county of Armagh where **apples** have been grown for thousands of years. Legend tells that Ireland's patron saint, St Patrick, planted an apple tree here.

Another famous apple tree is the one in Woolsthorpe in Lincolnshire that Isaac Newton sat under. He was struck by a falling apple and this, according to Voltaire, was the inspiration Newton needed to understand the force of gravity.

Gravity plays a vital role in cricket, and this takes us to our final tree, in Kent. A **lime** tree used to lie inside the field of play at the St Lawrence Ground in Canterbury and special scoring rules were drawn up to accommodate it. The tree, weakened by rot, was felled by high winds in 2005 but traditionalists rejoiced when a new lime tree was planted in its place.

A FLORAL TRIBUTE

The British Isles were once known for their wildflower meadows, but intensive farming has destroyed most of these tranquil havens and many people are now so detached from nature that the nation's flowers go unrecognized. It wasn't always this way, and here we look at the role of flowers in our history and culture before detailing some of Britain's favourite flowers.

Flowers were important to our pagan ancestors and many of their customs were kept even after the British Isles adopted Christianity. The strewing of flowers and petals was a feature of both weddings and funerals, and churches were decorated with flowers and fresh greenery at summer festivals. Clergymen even wore wreaths during services, and in 1405 the Bishop of London was garlanded in red roses to celebrate a feast for St Paul.

This all changed during the Reformation as Protestantism removed, often violently, the sensual and decorative elements of Christianity. Flowers disappeared from churches for hundreds of years and only returned in the nineteenth-century, possibly through people following trends set by Queen Victoria. Until this shift in fashion the laying of wreaths was discouraged as 'heathen'.

As flowers returned to churches in the nineteenth and twentieth centuries, they started to disappear from the countryside. Now, wildflower meadows have to be carefully husbanded by conservationists if they are to survive. Some native flower species are endangered, although the County Flowers scheme aims to preserve them and now each county in Britain has adopted a wild flower as an emblem.

Although **daisy** is a popular girl's name the word originated from Old English where it meant 'day's eye' – a reference to the appearance of the flower, which opens in the morning and closes in the evening. Traditionally, the daisy is an emblem of deceit, and in Shakespeare's *Hamlet* the queen is given daisies by Ophelia to remind her that 'her light and fickle love ought not to expect constancy in her husband'.

The **rose** is an emblem of England, and the red-and-white Tudor rose is a symbol of England uniting after the Wars of the Roses between the House of York (whose symbol was a white rose) and the House of Lancaster (symbolized by a red rose). An 'English rose' is not always a flower, however, and describes an attractive young woman of delicate complexion.

The national symbol of Wales, aside from the leek, is the **daffodil**. They are a welcome spring visitor where, in Shakespeare's words, they 'take the winds of March with beauty'. The daffodil, sometimes fancifully called the 'daffodowndilly', is one of Britain's favourite flowers and inspired one of the nation's best-loved poems when William Wordsworth saw 'a host of golden daffodils' as he 'wandered lonely as a cloud'.

Wordsworth was later inspired by a flower called **love-lies-bleeding**, an amaranth, as were earlier English poets John Milton and Edmund Spenser. Perhaps they were all taken by the classical myth that the amaranth was an immortal flower.

A useful flower for farmers is the **shepherd's sundial**, named because it opens at just after seven in the morning and closes at a shade after two. It does not open at all when bad weather is imminent and so its other name is the **shepherd's weatherglass**.

London pride has been the name for a number of plants but it is now applied to a small red-and-white flower also known as 'none-so-pretty'. A Victorian clergyman, Bishop How, wrote a poem rebuking the poor flower for having the sin of pride. When told that it wasn't the flower that was proud but Londoners of the flower, he penned a second poem by way of an apology.

UNDER THE
WEATHER

Samuel Johnson, the famous dictionary compiler, once noted:
'When two Englishmen meet, their first talk is of the weather.'
The British Isles' location, between dry continental air and moist
air from the Atlantic, leads to the sort of unsettled weather the
country enjoys, endures, and loves talking about. After a look at
Britain's contribution to weather forecasting we will describe some
of the weather conditions characteristically found on these islands
and the names given to them.

The United Kingdom is surrounded by water, and so seafaring
has always been a way of life. During the era of Empire and
exploration Britain had the largest military and merchant navies
in the world. Men and cargoes could easily perish on storm-tossed
seas so in 1854 the **Meteorological Office** was founded as a service
to mariners. Within a few years the first gale warnings were issued
and then, a few years later, weather forecasts.

The Met Office (as it is now known) was founded by Robert
FitzRoy, whose other claim to fame is captaining HMS *Beagle* on
which a young Charles Darwin gathered research vital to his work
on evolution. FitzRoy was honoured in 2002 by having a shipping
area, the one west of the Bay of Biscay, named after him. Each day
the conditions in FitzRoy and the other thirty areas are reported
in the **Shipping Forecast**, a four-times daily broadcast on BBC
Radio 4 that is essential listening for sailors.

Another admiral was Francis Beaufort. An Irishman,
he served with the Royal Navy in whose service he devised the
Beaufort Scale which categorizes wind speeds from 0 (calm)
to 12 (hurricane force) and which is still used to this day.

Beaufort and FitzRoy both lived the latter half of their
lives in Victorian Britain, a place that was no stranger to fog.
During the Industrial Revolution the capital became infamous
for its thick, yellowy fogs which were initially given the name

'**London particulars**'. The first evidence for this term's use is in Charles Dickens' *Bleak House*. Dickens might also have been familiar with this noxious fog's other name: the '**pea-souper**', an appropriate moniker considering the fog's thickness and colour.

Such thick fogs occurred well after Victorian times, and early in the twentieth century the word **smog** was coined by Henry Des Voeux of the Coal Abatement Society. He campaigned to improve the air quality of Britain's polluted cities, two of which, Edinburgh and London, had earned the respective nicknames '**Auld Reekie**' and '**The Smoke**'. Inhabitants of Middlesbrough, an industrial town in north-east England, are still known as '**smoggies**' despite the improved quality of the UK's atmosphere since the Clean Air Act of 1956.

Less troublesome are the sea mists that roll in from the North Sea onto the east coast of Scotland and north-east England. Known as **haar** (a Dutch word), this mist is a feature of early summer and is also known in England as **sea fret**.

A wetter mist, found in upland areas north of the border, is **Scotch mist**. A combination of drizzle and thick mist, it has achieved proverbial status in the saying: 'A Scotch mist wets an Englishman to the skin'. This weather might also be described as **dreich** which, when intoned by a Scotsman who has forgotten his umbrella, perfectly sums up weather that is grey, wet, and miserable.

A lighter Scottish drizzle is called a **smirr**, which might be related to the Dutch word *smoor* (mist), while in England a similar light drizzle is called **mizzle**. Such drizzly and misty weather may not appeal to some but, according to writer Charles Kingsley, it is character-building: ''Tis the hard grey weather breeds hard English men.'

WORK

BRITAIN AT WORK

The British class system traditionally divided the population into three groups: the upper class, the middle class, and the working class. It is quite odd that the third group should be called the 'working class', when you might logically expect it to be called the 'lower class'. But the implication is clear: work is conceived of as a thing engaged in by the those on lowest rung of society, the people who don't have either the financial resources to live a life of leisure or the privilege of belonging to one of the professions (such as teaching or the church) that allows you not to get your hands dirty.

The role of the working class in Britain was to provide fodder for the nation's factories, farms, mills, and mines. The bleak living conditions endured by this group were memorably described by George Orwell in his classic 1937 book *The Road to Wigan Pier*, although others took a harsher view, depicting the urban poor as feckless and sodden with cheap drink. The proverbial expression had it that 'drink is curse of the working classes', but George Bernard Shaw neatly turned this around when he said that 'work is the curse of the drinking classes'.

By the 1960s Britain had become a more egalitarian society and the grinding poverty that Orwell had witnessed thirty years earlier had largely disappeared. The working class now became more confident as its preoccupations with football, music, and beer were embraced by the nation as a whole, and John Lennon famously sang that 'a working-class hero is something to be'.

In recent decades the structure of the working population has changed. Britain's manufacturing industries have declined and the service sector has flourished. Fewer jobs entail hard physical labour, and people are more likely to work in call centres, food outlets, or shops. In 1997 Labour politician John Prescott said, 'We are all middle class now'.

We may have less physically demanding jobs these days, but unfortunately we still do have to go to work, and for many of us everything we do has to be fitted in around our working day. In 2011 Nick Clegg coined the term 'alarm-clock Britain' to describe the mass of people who work long hours and struggle to maintain a decent standard of living.

In this section of the book we clock in and take a look at how work has affected our lives and our language. We look at some traditional occupations and see how these can still be encountered in common British surnames, and we look at how changing working practices have been a constant source of new words. We also look at the pervasive influence of jargon (often imported from the USA) in the modern workplace – a practice that has attracted almost universal opprobrium but which shows no sign of abating. We then take a close look at two industries that have had contributed greatly to the vocabulary of modern English. The banking industry has a long history in Britain, but since many banks have been bailed out by the taxpayer we now take a closer interest in the financial sector as we wonder when we are going to get our money back. The computing industry is a relative newcomer in comparison, but there is no doubt that the introduction of computers has had a huge effect on the way that we work – and on our language – in recent years. Finally, we take a historical look at how British workers have attempted to improve their lot, and the conflicts – and words – that have arisen as a result.

JUST THE JOB

Working from nine to five is a relatively new way to make a living. Here we look at employment down the years in the British Isles, from the medieval serfs who were unable to leave their master's land to the modern 'workshifting' employees who can work wirelessly wherever and whenever they choose.

In the Middle Ages work meant agricultural labour. Peasants worked the land and there were two types. **Serfs** were unfree and effectively owned by the Lord of the Manor, while **yeomen** owned relatively small areas of land. In the fourteenth century the Black Death resulted in a dramatic drop in population that gave the remaining serfs the bargaining power that brought the feudal system to an end.

Most people lived in villages where each craft was practised by one person. Some people came to be known by their profession, for example Smith (blacksmith) and Cooper (barrel-maker). Some trades had different names in different regions, so a person who fulled cloth got the name Fuller in eastern England, Tucker in the south-west, Walker in the north, and Bowker in Lancashire.

In the early modern period trades were hierarchical, and made up of apprentices, journeymen, and masters who formed **guilds** to protect their interests. Much of this system came to an end during the Industrial Revolution when machines either replaced or de-skilled workers. Some workers, fearing for their livelihoods, destroyed their machines. One group, the **Luddites** (perhaps named after one of their number, Ned Ludd), became so well known that the word Luddite is still used to mean someone opposed to new technology.

Working conditions in the early nineteenth century were appalling for many workers. Long hours and lack of safety characterized most jobs. However, a combination of social reformers, trade unions, and a few enlightened employers improved the lot of the working man and woman, and paid holidays and weekends off came to be expected.

The twentieth century saw the rise of the **commuter**. Keen to escape city pollution (before the Clean Air Act of 1956 improved matters), many **white-collar workers** migrated to the gentler suburbs. In outer London this became known as the **commuter belt** or **Metroland**, an area served by the Metropolitan Railway and evoked in poetry by John Betjeman.

Britain's railway network abolished local time and introduced standard time across the country. Clocks were set to Greenwich Mean Time and workers were **clocking on** as factory whistles sounded simultaneously around the country. **Clockwatching** became common just before lunch and home time, and the **tea break**, the most important right of any British worker, became enshrined in the working day and heaven help any **jobsworth** who tried to have it shortened.

New technology has recently abolished many of Britain's familiar working traditions. The tea lady and her tea trolley have been replaced by coffee machines and the water cooler. Most people do their own typing and administration, so the typing pool has disappeared, and the nine-to-five working day has been replaced by flexible working hours.

Now the working day starts before office hours as people check their email on the train by smartphone. Lengthy breaks are discouraged. Food and drink is consumed 'al desko' and breakfast has become 'deskfast'. People sit in soulless open-plan offices ('cube farms') although workers in more creative industries might be found in a 'lifestyle office' where 'relaxation zones' are found and 'dress-down Friday' is every day of the week.

Employers praise '**flexible working**' (short-term contracts, freelancing, unpaid internships), but employees call it 'insecurity'. The underemployed dream of more work, while the full-timers struggle with their 'work-life balance'. In Britain these days the 'dream job', it seems, remains just that – a dream.

THINKING OUTSIDE THE BOX

Going forward, our mission statement will be to proactively cascade key step-changes in **management-speak** *from our provider vehicle (this book) to its stakeholders (you, the readers).*

Although it is tempting to assume that the impenetrable English used by businesspeople is a recent phenomenon, it should be noted that jargon has been irritating people in Britain for hundreds of years. Words such as 'jargonist' and 'jargonize' were coined long before the invention of flipcharts and Powerpoint.

Perhaps the worst type of jargon is **euphemism**. In the 1930s some British left-wing intellectuals were happy to describe Bolshevik atrocities against peasants as the 'pacification' of the Russian countryside, while boffins advising the wartime government described the targeting of residential areas by Bomber Command as the 'de-housing' of German workers.

In the workplace, euphemism pollutes the language of firing in particular. Terms such as 'downsizing', 'rightsizing' (not so 'right' for the people losing their job), and 'shrinking the headcount' are little comfort for the unfortunate employees who have been 'transitioned out'. Laid-off staff, if they are lucky, will receive a letter that 'wishes them well in their future endeavours'. Unlucky ones will be told by text message as they find themselves locked out their office.

Hiring is a more pleasant business, but the language is just as ugly. A surplus of suffixes is employed to describe the ideal candidate: 'results-driven', 'customer-focused', 'client-centred', and so on. Someone 'tasked' with a particularly soul-destroying job must be 'passionate' about it, no matter how tedious the work.

Problems do not exist in the modern workplace, only 'challenges'. People don't just 'meet' challenges, they 'take ownership' of them. Sporting analogies, usually imported from American sports, abound. Colleagues don't meet, they 'touch base'; managers are expected to 'play hardball' in negotiations;

and staff must 'step up to the plate' to deal with a problem, especially if it's a 'game-changing' one.

Big business is not the only serial offender against the English language. The people who carry out such simple tasks as filling in potholes and emptying bins are just as guilty. Indeed, the Local Government Association recently compiled a long list of terms it wanted to ban council staff from using. The public, not surprisingly, were getting confused by such gems as 're-baselining', 'benchmarking', and 'predictors of beaconicity'.

Central government is just as bad. When cabinet ministers talk to one another this is said to constitute 'joined-up government', while any public-sector body that achieves slightly more than mediocrity is a 'centre of excellence'.

The BBC was once regarded as a bastion of correct English with its motto of 'Nation shall speak peace unto nation', but the corporation has become infamous for its own brand of mystifying management jargon: **Birtspeak**. Coined by satirical magazine *Private Eye* in honour of John Birt (Director-General of the BBC in the 1990s), Birtspeak occurs most often in internal communications and job advertisements. For example, someone with the impressive-sounding job title of 'Category Manager Logistics Ground Transport' has the job of booking taxis.

Jargon is everywhere, but what can plain speakers do to combat it? They could run a '**jargon filter**' program that automatically deletes emails containing the user's least favourite jargon terms. Or they could enliven boring meetings with a game of '**buzzword bingo**' where jargon terms are crossed out until someone gets a 'full house'.

Finally, if jargon really offends it could be sent to the **Plain English Campaign**, an organization that fights 'gobbledygook, jargon, and misleading public information'. Its eagerly awaited 'Golden Bull' and 'Foot in Mouth' awards are an opportunity for the public to exact revenge against the worst of Britain's jargonistas.

BANK STATEMENT

Britain has been one of the world's leading financial centres for many years. Here we look at high finance over the centuries, from the early days when banking was considered a sin, to more recent times when our big banks needed bailing out.

Banking developed in the Middle Ages. Until they were expelled from England by Edward I in 1291, Jewish people were the chief moneylenders in England since they, unlike Christians, were not forbidden from charging interest. Italian merchants then took over banking, but only after a dispensation from the Pope.

The **Bank of England** was created in 1694, and a year later the **Bank of Scotland** was founded. When Scotland and England came together to form Great Britain the age of Empire began in earnest and banking was at the heart of it.

It was not just empire-builders who required funds. At the end of the following century **building societies** formed to cater for the more modest needs of savers and homeowners, while the chief purpose of **friendly societies** was as a benefit club in times of illness.

Britain became a world leader in banking in the nineteenth century when the Empire was at its peak, but in the following century two world wars and a depression put the country's finances under huge strain. Eventually the pound was supplanted by the dollar as the world's favourite currency and economic supremacy passed from Britain to the USA.

Although the 1960s are remembered fondly for other reasons, the decade was not so good for the nation's finances. International financiers disliked Britain's spiralling inflation and high levels of public spending and speculated against the pound. Labour politicians denounced these financiers as the '**gnomes of Zurich**', but in 1967 the government had to relent and devalue sterling. Prime Minister Harold Wilson told us that the 'pound in your pocket' would retain the same purchasing power, but few were convinced.

A combination of inflation and stagnation that the Conservative politician Iain Macleod dubbed **stagflation** plagued Britain in the early 1970s. Some executives tried to get round the government's anti-inflationary measures by awarding themselves secret tax-free bonuses, a scam Prime Minister Edward Heath famously called the 'unacceptable face of capitalism'.

Since the 1980s the City of London (Britain's financial sector) has grown as manufacturing has shrunk. **Deregulation** was the watchword in the 1980s and the **Big Bang** changed the way business was done as new technology was introduced. Privatization of state-owned utilities created millions of new share-owners. However, some of the shine was taken off 'popular capitalism' following two particularly black days. **Black Monday** in 1987 saw a huge fall in share values, and five years later **Black Wednesday** saw currency speculators profit as the pound was bundled out of the European Exchange Rate Mechanism.

The City quickly recovered from the setback. A long boom, based on easy credit and 'light-touch regulation', began. Cheap foreign labour kept inflation low and the boom was dubbed by the Governor of the Bank of England the '**NICE decade**' (of non-inflationary consistent expansion).

But it all came to a sorry end around 2007 with a **credit crunch** and a subsequent financial crash. Britain's banks had lent too freely, especially to people who couldn't pay the money back, and some needed huge **bailouts** from the taxpayer. Huge bonuses (despite low profits or even losses) mean that 'banker bashing' is now all the rage and even the City's regulator called some aspects of banking 'socially useless'. The Governor of the Bank of England has now promised a '**SOBER decade**' (of savings, orderly budgets, and equitable rebalancing). That's bankers' jargon for tighten your belts and hope for the best.

OK COMPUTER?

Britain has played an important role in the history of the computer. Here we look at Britain's contribution to computing and how computers have changed the way we work.

Steve Wozniak, one of Apple's co-founders, once joked: 'Never trust a computer you can't throw out a window.' He was not talking about the original computers, however, as the word was first used to mean 'a person who makes calculations'. Later, the Industrial Revolution made it possible for machines to make complicated calculations, and Charles Babbage's **difference engine** and **analytical engine**, although never fully built, anticipated some features of the modern computer.

One British machine that was built and did take the place of humans was the **Colossus**, the world's first electronic, programmable computer. Little was known about this computer until fairly recently, as its role in deciphering encrypted German radio messages during World War II was hushed up for decades. Indeed, after hostilities Churchill ordered the ten Colossus computers at the Bletchley Park deciphering station to be broken up in order to keep their workings secret.

For several decades after the war computers remained vast and expensive machines. Indeed, IBM's Thomas Watson once predicted: 'I think there is a world market for maybe five computers.' He was wrong. The microchip reduced both size and cost and eventually computers found their way into many businesses. The next development was the personal computer and Britain was at the forefront in the early 1980s with machines such as the **Sinclair ZX81** and the **BBC Micro** finding their way into homes and classrooms. But opportunities for expansion were missed and California's Silicon Valley became the home of the PC.

In the 1990s PCs were slow, unable to do more than one thing at a time, and prone to crashing. Error messages frequently popped up on screens and your firm's IT department might respond to problems by asking, 'Have you tried switching it off and on?' Bewildered users sometimes resorted to 'percussive maintenance' (hitting the computer).

At the end of the decade mistrust of computers reached a peak as the **millennium bug** threatened anything with a microchip and managers rushed to make office hardware 'Y2K-compliant'. But when January 2000 arrived the bug hadn't bitten and people wondered if disaster had been averted by heroic IT staff or if the threat had been overstated.

By now the creation of the **World Wide Web**, pioneered by Briton Tim Berners-Lee, had increased the usefulness of computers dramatically. A combination of broadband internet and more powerful and user-friendly computers meant that Britons soon couldn't live without their PCs. The online world is now no longer mockingly dismissed as the '**interweb**' and adeptness with technology is not evidence of 'geekdom'.

Computers killed off the typing pool, email is quicker and more reliable than the post, and teleconferencing reduces the need for early-morning shuttles. But increased communication also has its downsides. Much of the working day is now spent reading emails, too much time is wasted watching 'Powerpointless' presentations, and portable, wireless devices mean that 'workshifting' (working wherever and whenever) is expected.

The workplace is sometimes not the best place for work and some have to 'work from home' to get any work done. Internet access can lead to the twin temptations of excessive social networking ('social notworking') or watching the latest viral videos. Security is also a problem. Filing cabinets were never mislaid but memory sticks and laptops can easily go AWOL.

These complaints aside, the computer has made work simpler and quicker – even if it has meant us starting the working day on the train (assuming we can get a seat) with our laptop.

EVERYBODY OUT!

In this section we put down our tools and look at **industrial relations** in Britain, from the early years of exploitation and paternalism, through to the General Strike and wartime cooperation, and then to a more recent era of workplace strife and lost national prestige.

During the Industrial Revolution farm labourers flooded into towns to find work in the new factories and foundries, but they found that the factory owners cared no more about their welfare than the landowners had done. Workers banded together against capitalism's worst excesses, and the Committee of the Useful Classes was an early council of trade unions. Some employers wanted such unions to be kept illegal and the **Tolpuddle Martyrs** – Dorset farm labourers who formed a union in 1834 – were sentenced to transportation to Australia. However, their sentences were annulled after a public outcry in trade unionism's first notable victory.

Some employers were more sympathetic. Robert Owen ran the mills at New Lanark near Glasgow along paternalistic lines, providing housing and education for his workers and their families. The Quakers who founded some of our best known confectionery companies were similarly philanthropic, and the Bourneville village built near Birmingham was a huge step forward in living conditions for working people.

As Britain continued to industrialize, the union movement grew and by the Edwardian era its political wing, the Labour Party, had sent its first MPs to Westminster.

The Bolshevik Revolution in Russia shocked Britain's ruling classes and in 1919 troops and tanks were sent to Glasgow to quell '**Red Clydeside**', a socialist movement centred in the city's shipbuilding industry. '**Bolshy**' then became used as an abusive term for workers who didn't know their place and was probably used frequently during the 1926 **General Strike**, when the unions took action together and 'not a penny off the pay, not a second on the day' was the miners' slogan. Ernest Bevin was one of the strike's leaders but he later served as a minister under Churchill during the Second World War, when capital and labour put aside their differences to defeat a common foe.

After the war, many industries were nationalized and the trade-union movement reached its peak. Full employment was achieved but a 'them and us' attitude dominated industrial relations. In the film *I'm All Right, Jack* Peter Sellers played an officious **shop steward** (union official) who was more interested in his union rule book than the success of the company he worked for. Strikes, restrictive practices, and absenteeism blighted the factory floor in the 1960s and the French even coined a name for it: *la maladie anglaise* (**the British disease**).

The decade of the 1970s became synonymous with industrial action. During a miners' strike electricity had to be rationed, there were power cuts, and industry worked a **three-day week**. **Beer and sandwiches** were served to union leaders during frequent crisis talks at Downing Street, and the term quickly came to mean 'negotiations'. In 1978–9 a **Winter of Discontent** saw the country paralysed by strikes and a prime minister unsympathetic to trade unions, Margaret Thatcher, was elected soon after.

Mrs Thatcher put a stop to **closed shops** (workplaces where union membership is mandatory), **flying pickets** (strikers who go from one site to another to make strikes more effective), and unplanned **wildcat strikes**. Her defeat of the miners after a lengthy strike in 1984–5 brought an end to the era where union leaders were known as 'barons'. Since then strikes have become fewer, many industries have moved abroad, and more workers describe themselves as 'white-collar'. Millions still feel the need to join unions, however, as employers have not entirely lost their ability to exploit their workers.

THE

ENGLISH

LANGUAGE

FROM ANGLO-SAXON TO TEXTSPEAK

It is quite an odd thought that the original speakers of English didn't come from England at all. The 'Angles' and 'Saxons' were two Germanic tribes who arrived in Britain in the fifth century AD (hired as mercenaries by the crumbling Roman Empire), and who liked it so much that they stayed, imposing their Anglo-Saxon language on the indigenous people.

Anglo-Saxon lies at the root of English, although over the centuries the language has changed in many ways. The first major development came as a result of the influence of Viking raiders in the ninth century, who brought their own words and were responsible for the names of many places in eastern England. Then in1066 the Normans invaded England, and the country now had two languages: the Anglo-Saxon of the common people and the Norman French of the ruling class. In time the English language absorbed thousands of words from the French, making it quite distinct from other Germanic languages and it giving it a unique richness of vocabulary.

But the language continued to evolve. The arrival of printing helped to establish some conventions for written language, while a vogue for borrowing words from Latin and Greek further expanded the vocabulary. Canonical works of literature – notably the King James Version of the Bible and the plays of Shakespeare – also shaped the way that people thought of English. Moreover, English continued to be influenced by other languages as Britain developed an overseas empire. By the twentieth century, English had outgrown its birthplace and spread all over the world, forming new varieties in North America, Australia, India, and elsewhere, which in turn fed back into the English spoken in the British Isles.

FROM ANGLO-SAXON TO TEXTSPEAK

In the earlier sections of this book we have been looking at English through the prism of our national culture, observing how the British way of life has introduced particular words into the language. In the following pages we now turn the spotlight onto the language itself, looking at its history, at some of its characteristic features, and at how it is likely to develop in the future.

We start at the beginning with the Anglo-Saxon roots of the language, observing how these can still be seen in our everyday vocabulary. From there we look at some factors that have influenced the way that English has developed over the centuries, including seminal works of literature, and also how Britain's nautical and military past has exerted a strong (and not always obvious) influence on our current vocabulary.

We then turn to look at some features that give the English language a continuing fascination for many of its users. The history of English has left it with an unusually rich stock of words and phrases, so that English-speakers have almost endless possibilities for expressing themselves in original and interesting ways, whether it is through proverbs, idioms, or euphemisms, or by exploiting wordplay for humorous purposes.

The language we use has a long history and a flourishing present. Its vocabulary continues to expand as advances in science and technology bring new words into circulation, and in recent years changes in communications technology have brought about a revolution in the way we express ourselves as conventional forms of writing are replaced by email, text messages, and tweets. The process of continuous change means that some words become old-fashioned and drop out of everyday use, but these are more than compensated for by the many new ones – some essential for modern communication, some merely playful – that spring up to take their place.

SAY IT IN ANGLO-SAXON!

Everybody knows what they mean when they talk about using **Anglo-Saxon** words. It's that blunt, no-nonsense type of language that says exactly what it means on the tin, often unblushingly using only four letters (although we won't go into that *just* yet).

So who were these Anglo-Saxons who had such a lasting influence on the way British people speak today? Were they just a bunch of ale-swilling, foul-mouthed roughnecks, determined to call a spade a shovel? No doubt plenty of them were, but without their input the English language would be lacking not only in pretty basic terms but some of our more colourful and cultured vocabulary too. You might be surprised to know that all of the very familiar words (shown in bold below) come to us from Anglo-Saxon.

What could be more basic than your own **body**, your very own **flesh** and **blood**? Well, from your **brain** to your **ankles**, your **breast** to your **back**, your **ear** to your **belly**, the Anglo-Saxons took charge of the naming of parts. Think about that, next time you make that gesture of celebration by raising your **arm** with your **hand** made into a **fist**.

They certainly liked their food and drink, not just **ale** and **beer** but **water** too. Being farmers with **acres** of land and green **fields**, they knew how to raise **corn** and **barley** as well as **goats**, **cows** and **bulls**, grow **apples** and **leeks**, and **bake** their own **bread**.

They gave names to the plants and animals that they saw all around them, as typical of the British countryside then as they are now, from the **ants** or **beetles** crawling on the ground to the **crows** and **geese** in the sky above, the humble **daisy** growing in the **grass** underfoot to the tallest **birch** or **ash** or **oak** festooned in green **leaves**. Maybe you have a **dog** or a **cat**, or if you're that bit more adventurous you might keep **bees**. If you keep **chickens**, you better watch out for that **fox**!

The whole course of a **man** or **woman**'s **life** can still be told in Anglo-Saxon, from the day you're **born** until the day you **die**. Whether your **day** is looking **good** or **bad**, no doubt you'd rather be **alive** than **dead**! You can go out and have **fun** with the **friends** you like to share a few **laughs** with. Who knows, today might be the day you meet the **girl** or **boy** of your dreams (Hi **darling**, how about a big **kiss**?). Or you might prefer to stay in the **house** in the bosom of your family, with your **mother** and **father**, especially if it's your **birthday**. Do you have **brothers** and **sisters**, or are you an only **child**? Maybe there's a family **wedding** happening soon. Who's the lucky **lady** that's going to be a **bride** and the **lad** who'll be her **bridegroom**?

And where would the art of British conversation be without being able to discuss the **weather**? How long is this **winter** going to last? Will the trains start running late if we get the wrong kind of **snow**? It might already be **spring** but it still looks like it's going to **rain**. Or is it **cold** enough for **sleet**? And then if the **wind** rises, will there be **hail**? Wait a minute! Isn't that the **sun** coming out from behind the **clouds** at last? Don't forget that British **summers** can be **hot** as well as **wet**! People are already starting to **sweat**. Wasn't there something in the news about a **drought** already?

The earliest Anglo-Saxon writing did not use the Roman alphabet, but a system of runes called **futhork**. Two of these runic letters, called thorn and wynn, were later used in the Roman alphabet alongside our familiar letters, but they were eventually replaced by 'th' and 'w' respectively.

WAXING BIBLICAL

In 1611 a new English translation of The Bible was published at the instigation of King James I. The language of this version has resonated throughout the English-speaking world for over 400 years. Even though the twentieth century saw new translations into more modern language, it is the sonorous, authoritative English of the '**King James Version**' that British people in particular instinctively turn to at times of great ceremony. The milestones of life – birth, marriage, and death – seem to be unsatisfyingly marked without a reading from this text, archaic as it may often sound to modern ears.

While Britain is far from being the monolithically Christian country of past centuries, and even amongst nominal Christians the habit of regular churchgoing has greatly declined, it seems that Biblical language is hardwired into the national consciousness. So many idioms and turns of phrase that spring almost automatically to mind are taken straight from the King James Bible, and many people who use them daily may be surprised to find that this is the case. This is the source of such expressions as **feet of clay**, **the apple of his eye**, **the salt of the earth**, **the powers that be**, and **den of thieves**.

Many of the proverbial phrases we use in conversation are versions of Biblical originals, if not direct quotations. When we say that **a leopard doesn't change his spots** we are paraphrasing the Book of Jeremiah (13: 23): 'Can the Ethiopian change his skin, or the leopard his spots?' Those who castigate others for failing to believe them by saying '**O ye of little faith**' are quoting the Gospel of Matthew (8: 25-27), and anyone who characterizes a confused situation as **the blind leading the blind** is harking back to Matthew 14: 14 ('Let them alone: they be blind leaders of the blind. And if the blind lead the blind, both shall fall into the ditch').

You might not realize it, but it's the Bible you are referencing when you quite naturally reach for phrases like **eat, drink and be merry**, **an eye for an eye**, **let there be light**, **no peace for the**

wicked, **kill the fatted calf**, **a still, small voice**, **seek and ye shall find**, **sufficient unto the day is the evil thereof**, **fight the good fight**, **keep the faith**, **how are the mighty fallen** … the list is endless!

When younger generations look at the many war memorials that are scattered all over the British Isles, especially those erected to honour the thousands who perished in World War I, they may wonder about the source of the wording '**Their name liveth for evermore**'. It is simply a shortened part of *Ecclesiasticus* 44:14 – 'Their bodies are buried in peace; but their name liveth for evermore.'

The King James Bible has always been an ideal quarry for writers seeking impressive-sounding titles for their work. With books such as *The Grapes of Wrath* and *East of Eden* (both by John Steinbeck), *The Sun Also Rises* (Ernest Hemingway), *The Seven Pillars of Wisdom* (TE Lawrence), *The Sound and the Fury* (William Faulkner), *The Golden Bowl* (Henry James), *Stranger in a Strange Land* (Robert Heinlein), and *Cities of the Plain* (Cormac McCarthy), we hear the unmistakable ring of the austere poetry of Jacobean language. And the book doesn't have to be deadly serious; Stephen Fry called a volume of autobiography *Moab is My Washpot*, an obscure reference lifted from Psalm 60. Even the Rolling Stones, notwithstanding their plea for sympathy for the Devil, were echoing St Paul's Letter to the Corinthians ('For now we see through a glass, darkly') when they called their 1969 compilation album *Through the Past, Darkly*.

SHAKESPEARE SAID IT FIRST

In the history of English literature no single writer has left such a mark on the language as **William Shakespeare**. Although the man himself died as long ago as 1616, his plays have never stopped being performed all over the English-speaking world. It's no wonder, then, that his influence on the way we speak and write is unparalleled. When you come across a popular, well-known, and memorable phrase in English, there is quite a good chance that Shakespeare said it first! To take only one of his plays, *Hamlet,* as an example, it is from there that we quote such immediately recognizable turns of phrase as:

- ❖ for this relief much thanks
- ❖ frailty, thy name is woman
- ❖ the primrose path
- ❖ neither a borrower nor a lender be
- ❖ to thine own self be true
- ❖ to the manner born
- ❖ a custom more honoured in the breach than the observance
- ❖ something is rotten in the state of Denmark
- ❖ murder most foul
- ❖ there are more things in heaven and earth, Horatio, (than are dreamt of in your philosophy)
- ❖ brevity is the soul of wit
- ❖ though this be madness, yet there is method in it
- ❖ what a piece of work is a man

- ❖ caviare to the general
- ❖ the play's the thing
- ❖ to be or not to be
- ❖ shuffle off this mortal coil
- ❖ the lady doth protest too much
- ❖ alas, poor Yorick
- ❖ the rest is silence

While perhaps not on the same scale as *Hamlet,* most of Shakepeare's plays have yielded phrases that have become almost proverbial.

When we talk about getting **a pound of flesh**, or assert that **it is a wise father that knows his own child**, and **the quality of mercy is not strained**, or demand **if you prick us, do we not bleed?** we are quoting from *The Merchant of Venice.*

Macbeth is the source of such phrases as **the milk of human kindness**, **is this a dagger which I see before me?**, **out, damned spot**, **all our yesterdays**, **one fell swoop**, as well as the much-quoted witches' spell that begins **'eye of newt, and toe of frog'**.

If you warn someone to **beware the ides of March**, or feel like shouting **cry 'Havoc!' and let slip the dogs of war**, you owe this to *Julius Caesar.* You might be fond enough of Latin to quote its memorable line *et tu, Brute* or you might admit **it was Greek to me**. It was here that Mark Antony first declaimed **friends, Romans, countrymen, lend me your ears** and called Caesar **the noblest Roman of them all**.

It's no accident that *Henry V* was made into a film in 1944 when, at the height of World War II, Britain was most in need of its ringing phrases of patriotism and fighting spirit, like **once more unto the breach**, **cry 'God for Harry! England and Saint George!'**, and **we happy few, we band of brothers**.

It was the eponymous hero of *Othello* who was tormented by jealousy (**the green-ey'd monster**), described himself as **one that lov'd not wisely but too well,** and lamented the fact that in murdering his wife Desdemona he **threw a pearl away richer than all his tribe**.

Pomp and circumstance, **sea change**, **salad days**, **more sinned against than sinning**, **my kingdom for a horse**, and **winter of (our) discontent** are all sayings that are taken from one or other of Shakespeare's plays, but even some of the names of characters have become inextricably woven into the language. Everyone knows what is meant when a man is called a **Romeo**, and what sort of person shows a **Falstaffian** attitude to life (someone who will **eat you out of house and home**, for one thing!). **Shylock** is still shorthand for a miser, and followers of female fashion will know how to accessorize with a **Juliet** cap.

Just like the King James Bible, the works of Shakespeare have provided thousands of other writers with resonant titles for their own works, and some of them might surprise you. Here's a short list:

- ❖ *Ill Met by Moonlight* by W Stanley Moss (from *A Midsummer Night's Dream*)

- ❖ *Under the Greenwood Tree* by Thomas Hardy (*As You Like It*)

- ❖ *Band of Brothers* by Stephen Ambrose (*Henry V*)

- ❖ *The Dogs of War* by Frederick Forsyth (*Julius Caesar*)

- ❖ *By the Pricking of my Thumbs* by Agatha Christie (*Macbeth*)

- ❖ *Something Wicked This Way Comes* by Ray Bradbury (*Macbeth*, the other half of the preceding title!)

- ❖ *A Heart So White* by Javier Marias (*Macbeth*)

- ❖ *Pomp and Circumstance* by Noel Coward (*Othello*)

- ❖ *The Winter of our Discontent* by John Steinbeck (*Richard III*)

- ❖ *Brave New World* by Aldous Huxley (*The Tempest*)

Films have also borrowed from The Bard of Avon, including *Where Eagles Dare, Heaven's Gate, The Evil that Men Do, What Dreams May Come,* and *To Be or Not To Be,* to name but a few, and TV gets in on the act with *The Darling Buds of May, To the Manor Born* (a pun in this case!), and *Band of Brothers.* Most people know that Agatha Christie's play *The Mousetrap* has had one of the longest-running chains of performances on record, but did you know that its title is taken from the 'play within a play' in *Hamlet*?

Many of the words we use in everyday speech were first recorded in print in a Shakespeare play. Some of these he probably coined himself, but even those he didn't wouldn't have been picked up if he hadn't given them popular exposure. This included things we might consider basic stuff, such as **accountant, affinity, amend, appliance, bedlam, brine, carouse, clamorous, confederacy, cuckold, deify, dismantle, drudge, element, enchant, enfranchise, envious, filch, gambol, indulgence, issue, livery, marvellous, murmur, office, paragon, peevish, pestilence, prattle, quaint, remembrance, saucy, schooling, surfeit, tidings, transgress, undo,** and **waggish.**

Considering he is Britain's most famous writer, it is remarkable that nothing at all is known of Shakespeare's activities in the seven years between 1585 and the performance of his earliest play in 1592. Suggestions as to his possible whereabouts in this period include that he was involved in a dissident Catholic group in Lancashire, that he worked as a country schoolmaster, and that he sailed around the world with Sir Francis Drake on *The Golden Hind.*

ANYONE FOR QUIDDITCH?

Shakespeare may be our best known writer, but there have been plenty of other British writers who have introduced new words. If the word they needed didn't exist already they just made it up!

We've all been guilty of unintentionally mixing up our words to form a **malapropism**, but did you know this word comes from a fictional character? This was Mrs Malaprop, in Richard Sheridan's play *The Rivals* (1775). The same century gave us **yahoo**, meaning a coarse or brutish person, which was coined by Jonathan Swift in his novel *Gulliver's Travels*.

The nineteenth century was a period when a great deal of 'nonsense' writing was popular, and this genre was highly productive of new words. Among its chief exponents was Lewis Carroll, author of *Alice's Adventures in Wonderland*, who gave us **chortle** and **galumph**, although some of his other coinages, like 'frabjous' didn't make it into wider use. Edward Lear's nonsense verse was full of words of his own invention, like 'slobaciously' or 'flumpetty' but the only one to survive in English dictionaries is **runcible** (for those who don't know, a runcible spoon is a cross between a fork and a spoon).

Often what seized the imagination of the general public was a particular person in a work of literature, to the extent that their names became shorthand for types of people. In *The Strange Case of Dr Jekyll and Mr Hyde* Robert Louis Stevenson portrayed a man with a personality so split into good and evil that each aspect of the same person existed as a separate character with his own name. To this day we still speak of someone capable of seemingly contrasting modes of behaviour as a **Jekyll-and-Hyde character**.

The eponymous hero of JM Barrie's *Peter Pan* was a 'boy who never grew up' and his name is still applied to a boyish or immature man, as well as to a **Peter Pan collar** on an item of clothing. Barrie invented the girl's name Wendy for another character in the same play, and it's from her that the **Wendy House** took its name.

Charles Dickens populated his novels with unforgettable characters, many of whose traits and foibles ensured that they would be remembered in the language. From Mr Pickwick we derive the adjective **Pickwickian**, meaning 'odd or unusual', and the eternal optimist and idler Mr Micawber lends his name to a **Micawberish** attitude (always expecting something good to turn up without making a personal effort). **Gamp**, an informal term for an umbrella, comes from Mrs Gamp in *Martin Chuzzlewit*, who was never seen without hers, and Ebenezer Scrooge, from *A Christmas Carol*, gave us another name for a miser.

In the twentieth century, one of the writers who contributed most new words to the language was George Orwell. In 1949 he published his novel, *Nineteen Eighty-Four*, a nightmarish vision of a near future under a totalitarian regime, in which he coined such words as **doublethink** (the deliberate blending of two conflicting beliefs), **newspeak** (deliberately ambiguous and misleading language) and the **thought police** (a group who monitor others for deviations from the accepted ways of thinking). With his phrase 'Big Brother is watching you' he anticipated a society in which the individual's every move would be watched, and this is nowadays applied to everything from surveillance cameras to reality television shows. No wonder his name was borrowed, in the adjective **Orwellian**, to describe a bleak view of the future!

Writers are still coining new words, of course, and one of the most recent to make it into dictionaries is **quidditch**, the name of the imaginary game invented by JK Rowling in her 'Harry Potter' novels.

IF YOU'LL PARDON
MY FRENCH!

The English language is always expanding its vocabulary. If there isn't already a word for something we're happy to invent one. But if that's too much like hard work why not simply borrow a word from another language and start using that? With our notoriously poor grasp of foreign tongues, once we start pronouncing it in a more British way it'll sound right at home!

Britain's nearest neighbour is of course France, so it's only natural that English has plenty of words of French origin. A lot of these came in with the Norman Conquest in 1066 but the process of borrowing has gone on ever since, especially in the fields of food and the arts.

Those of us who aspire to be a **gourmet**, or at least a **bon viveur**, will certainly know one end of a **canapé** from another. We'll enter our favourite **restaurant** with a friendly nod to the **maître d'hôtel**, then cruise effortlessly through a **menu** (whether it's **à la carte** or **table d'hôte**), from **hors d'oeuvres** to **liqueurs**.

If you're a **connoisseur** of creative endeavour, even a little **avant-garde**, you'll find the French probably gave us the terms with which to show off about it. You might be into **Art Nouveau** or **ballet**, or maybe **haute couture** is your preferred **genre**; no matter, as long as you can recognize a **tour de force** or **pièce de résistance** when you see one.

Not all of our French borrowings are so highfalutin of course. Our tiny tots may be dropped off at the local **crèche** while we head off to work **en masse**. Do you have **carte blanche** to do what you like, or are you presented with a **fait accompli**? When you check in to your holiday **hotel** or **chalet** you'll be glad that **en suite** facilities are now **de rigueur**, even if the sameness of the **décor** gives you a feeling of **déjà vu**.

Other languages also get a chance to lend us some terms. Where would we be without Italian when we want to order the latest trendy variation on coffee? We'd have to forgo our **espressos**, **cappuccinos**, and **lattes** if we couldn't tell the **barista** exactly what we need. And that's before we get into the many varieties of **pasta**. It's a **spaghetti** junction out there! When you're at the **opera**, savouring some fashionable **soprano's** rendition of your favourite **aria**, you'll know you're truly experiencing the **dolce vita**.

Lots of us have been to Spain and picked up a smattering of the Spanish language, but you don't have to be an **aficionado** of Iberian culture to enjoy a visit to the **cafeteria**. Why not break out the **sherry**? Any excuse for a **fiesta**! Have you ever been rendered **incommunicado** by your friends? Maybe it's because you came over all **macho** when you were in the **plaza**. If you enjoy dancing the **rumba** or the **paso doble**, never forget that it takes two to **tango**!

If you call a period of sustained activity a **blitz**, then it's German you're borrowing from. The same applies if you like to talk about being in tune with the **zeitgeist**. If you have a **doppelgänger** you might regard anything unfortunate that happens to them with a degree of **schadenfreude**. (Perhaps their **dachshund** did something unpleasant outside the **kindergarten**.) Do you enjoy a **hamburger**, or prefer to buy your food from a **delicatessen**? Have a few **pretzels** with your **lager**!

All of these borrowed words and more are there for us to use, as long as we have the **chutzpah** (and that last one's from Yiddish).

BRITANNIA RULES THE WAVES!

The British have always been a sea-going nation – as the inhabitants of one big island and a lot of smaller ones, it comes with the territory. Throughout the history of 'this island race' the surrounding waters have been a source of food and a medium of communication, trade, and exploration. It was sailing ships that carried our empire builders, and the Royal Navy that protected them. It's hardly surprising, then, that a great deal of nautical vocabulary has become fixed in the English language, even when it's landlubbers that are using it!

The sea itself is known by many names. To some it's **the briny**; to others **the drink**. Sailors often saw it as being ruled over by a spirit or devil, whom they christened **Davy Jones**, and therefore, if you were unfortunate enough to be in a ship that sank you were said to be going to **Davy Jones's locker**.

The general population could be suspicious of sailors, who were sometimes seen as too free-and-easy and given to uproarious behaviour when on shore, and gave them labels like **old salt**, **old sea dog**, or **Jack Tar**. They might face a **broadside** of criticism, but their often colourful nautical language maintains a wide currency.

The time when sailing ships were dominant is long over, but it's surprising to note how many everyday expressions derive from those days. Let's get **under way**. Everyone knows that if you are **taken aback** you are startled or disconcerted, but did you know that the expression literally refers to a ship being brought to a halt when the wind is blowing from directly in front of it? Similarly, you won't make much progress when something **takes the wind from your sails**. If you know what you are doing, you are said to **know the ropes**, but if you are a little too drunk, you might be **three sheets in the wind** ('sheets' in this case being the ropes used to control a sail). Best to go for moderation when you **splice the mainbrace** (that is, have an alcoholic drink).

'On board' of course means on or onto a vessel, but if you **take something on board** you accept it. If, on the other hand, it **goes by the board**, it is got rid of (as in chucked over the side). We've all experienced great enthusiasm for one thing or another, but it doesn't do to **go overboard**, does it? You don't want to find yourself **all at sea**!

If you're expecting trouble, it might occur to you to **batten down the hatches** (originally meaning to secure a ship against a coming storm). Afterwards, if you tidy the place up, you are said to **clear the decks**, and if you do this thoroughly you sort it out **from stem to stern**. Are you in cramped quarters … **no room to swing a cat**? Don't worry, no animals will be harmed! The 'cat' in question is the 'cat o' nine tails', a fearsome whip formerly used to punish unfortunate sailors, which would need enough space for the wielder to give it a good swing.

When you're out on the ocean you might long for a sight of dry land but you've got to be careful: you don't want to **run aground** and be left **high and dry**. If that does happen, you'll be left waiting for high water to **tide you over**. With nothing much to do, the crew will probably start gossiping amongst themselves, exchanging the latest **scuttlebutt** which was the water barrel on deck where everyone went for drink – just like today's water cooler.

ALL PRESENT AND CORRECT

The great English lexicographer Samuel Johnson famously said that 'every man thinks meanly of himself for not having been a soldier'. Whatever the truth of this sweeping assertion, the fact remains that the military has had a demonstrable influence on the lives of Britons with no direct experience of it – not least in our everyday language.

Do you don a **Balaclava** when the weather turns icy? Perhaps you weren't aware that this natty knitted headpiece is named after the prototype first adopted by Victorian British soldiers at the siege of the Russian city of the same name during the Crimean War. Perhaps as they wore theirs they dreamed of going home to **Blighty**, a name for Britain that came out of the British Army in India. If it's merely a bit wet, rather than freezing, you might be content to wear a **trench coat** (named after those worn by army officers in the First World War). **Camouflage** trousers go in and out of fashion, but the style is a copy of the patterned clothing worn by soldiers in the field to help them pass unnoticed by the enemy.

Many of us have friends or relations with army connections, whether they are regular **squaddies** or spend their weekends training with the **Terries** (Territorial Army). If they're in a Guards regiment, we might even have seen them on parade in their **bearskin** helmets.

But most of the military-influenced language we use every day is not about army things at all, but more in the way of metaphorical expressions. When you want to have a look at a place or weigh up a situation, it's always best to **have a recce** (do some reconnaissance). If you are brave enough to make a suggestion that might meet with objections, you are often said to **stick your head above the parapet** or **run it up the flagpole and see who salutes**. New ideas run the risk of undergoing a **barrage** of criticism, but if you can deal with the **flak**, you might just **carry the day**, as long as you don't give in to the temptation to go **AWOL**. It often depends on what the **top brass** think about it, but if you're one of the **big guns** your opinion will be valued.

The Second World War gave us the term **blitz** (from the German *blitzkrieg* meaning 'lightning war') and nowadays we use it to mean any session of concentrated effort, like a cleaning blitz. That conflict is also the origin of **gone for a Burton** (meaning 'broken, finished, or dead'), which was originally RAF slang used when a pilot didn't return from a sortie. When something new is invented in the field of science we still talk about it being the brainchild of **boffins**, a terms that was originally military slang.

More modern conflicts have also left their mark on our language. Do you like to go for a **yomp** across the hills in your spare time? Before the Falklands War in the 1980s popularized the term you would have called it something else. When someone becomes a casualty through the actions of their own side we call them victims of **friendly fire** (a contradiction in terms if there ever was one). And people who get hurt as a consequence when we try to damage an enemy are dismissed by the callous as **collateral damage**.

And we've all seen contestants in popular television reality and talent shows doing their utmost to be accepted for **boot camp**, but would they be so keen if it still had its original meaning of a military training establishment?

GREAT MINDS
THINK ALIKE

The British love their **proverbs**. There's nothing like repeating a wise old saw to make you seem as if you've been around and know a thing or two. But how do the nation's favourite proverbs express the national character?

The British are traditionally said to be very much in favour of fair play and we like to think of ourselves as sticking up for the underdog, and this attitude spawns proverbs like **give credit where credit is due**, **give a dog a bad name and hang him**, **pick on someone your own size**, **play up and play the game**, and **every dog has its day**.

We're a pretty tolerant bunch as a rule; we're happy to let others get on with their lives as long as they don't annoy anyone else! That's why we say **live and let live**, **it takes all sorts to make a world**, **to each his own**, **two wrongs don't make a right** and **one man's meat is another man's poison**.

And where would the art of British conversation be without being able to complain about the weather? We all know that **it never rains but it pours** and **it's an ill wind that blows nobody any good**. You have to **make hay while the sun shines** but, after all, everybody knows **one swallow doesn't make a summer**. Once we've finished grousing about wintry weather we soon get fed up with summer heat and drought – **you can have too much of a good thing**!

When you look at all the proverbs that urge us to be cautious in what we do, you would be forgiven for thinking that the Brits are a rather timid lot. We're always advising others to **look before you leap**, **it's better to be safe than sorry**, that **fools rush in where angels fear to tread**, and **the grass is always greener on the other side**. When **all that glitters isn't gold** and **a fool and his money are soon parted**, doesn't it make more sense not to **put all your eggs in one basket**? Don't be rash and rush into things: **let sleeping**

dogs lie and **least said soonest mended**. In **once bitten, twice shy** there speaks the wisdom born from hard-won experience, so **marry in haste and repent at leisure**, and if you must hook up with a partner and start a family, **don't throw out the baby with the bathwater**.

But, just when you're writing us off as cowardy custards, back come the British with a completely contradictory set of maxims – yes, being contradictory is a national characteristic too – which tend to show us in a more adventurous light. **Fortune favours the brave**, we proclaim, and **he who hesitates is lost**. When **you might as well be hung for a sheep as a lamb**, it's a clear case of **in for a penny, in for a pound**. Don't you realize that **time and tide wait for no man**? So if **there's no time like the present**, you had better **strike while the iron is hot** and **if you don't succeed, try, try, try again**!

We're a home-loving nation at heart, and well appreciate the simple joys of domesticity. **Home is where the heart is**, we like to say, and **an Englishman's home is his castle**. But whatever you do, try to get on with your neighbours: **people who live in glass houses shouldn't throw stones**!

So British proverbs show how our **great minds think alike** … but then again … **fools seldom differ**!

WHY NOT GET IT OFF YOUR CHEST?

As languages go, English – especially as it is spoken in Great Britain – is particularly rich in **idioms**. On these pages we highlight some British idioms, but what exactly is an idiom **when it's at home**? **It's not rocket science**: an idiom is simply an expression made up of a series of words, in which the meaning of the expression can't be worked out from the meanings of the individual words. Well, is that **as clear as mud**? Let's look at an example. If someone tells you that **it's raining cats and dogs**, this is not to say that if you stick your head out of your window you are likely to be walloped on the head by a rapidly descending Rottweiler or Siamese. No, it's just a colourful way of letting you know that it's raining heavily.

The commonness of idioms in English is one of the features of the language that is said to make it particularly tricky for non-native speakers to become truly fluent in it. You can't *decode* an idiom by trying to analyse its different elements; you just have to learn what they mean by becoming familiar with them (get to **know the ropes**). We've started with an idiom relating to that perennial topic of British conversation, the weather, so why not have a look at a few more in that line?

The rain could be **coming down in buckets** or maybe even **coming down in stair-rods**; if it's very cold it could be **no weather for brass monkeys** (cold enough to freeze off the poor creatures', ahem, extremities), or if by any chance it's actually hot and sunny you might hear a person (or a newspaper headline) exclaim **what a scorcher**! You can **get cold feet** at any season though – that simply means to become scared or have second thoughts about some undertaking.

But not all idioms that take their imagery from the weather are actually *about* the weather. Take for example **under the weather** which means feeling slightly ill, or **make heavy weather** of something, meaning to make it seem more difficult than it is. Someone who deserts you when you're in trouble is a **fair-weather friend**, and if you **keep your weather eye open**, you're being alert and watchful.

While it can be windy in Britain, in the right doses this can be seen as being refreshing (it can **blow the cobwebs away**) and to be **bright and breezy** is to be cheerful. But if someone tells you that you **blow hot and cold**, they are criticizing you for continually changing your mind.

The British are famous for their love of animals, especially their domestic pets, and the language is full of references to them. You might think you know what constitutes a pet's diet, but **a dog's breakfast** has nothing to do with it: it means a mess. But, contrarily enough, if you're all dressed up **like a dog's dinner** this means you look very smart. If you own a dog you might wonder what's so different about these meals! **Dog eat dog** doesn't suggest canine cannibalism but is used to describe a situation of extreme and ruthless competitiveness. If you **go to the dogs** you are facing ruin, but if you want to **see a man about a dog** you're letting people know that you're going to the toilet. You don't want to end up **in the doghouse**, though, as this means you've annoyed someone.

Let's not forget the cats while we're at it. If you reveal a secret you are said to **let the cat out of the bag** and something that's reckoned to be the very best is **the cat's pyjamas** (or it could be **the bee's knees** or even **the dog's bollocks** – who knows why?).

If a task is for you to carry out alone, **it's your pigeon**, and if you put all you've got into it, you're said to **go the whole hog**. **Monkey business** is something mischievous or dishonest, which might be detected by someone who claims to **smell a rat**. You might be **sick as a parrot** if you discover that it's been going on **for donkey's years** (a very long time).

Convivial Brits like to mark every social occasion with a few drinks – any excuse to **wet your whistle!** – but you don't always have to **push the boat out**. There's bound to be someone who starts telling risqué stories or jokes that are a bit **off-colour** or too **near the knuckle**. If you do happen to overindulge (have **one over the eight**) you might find yourself a bit drunk and be **half seas over** or **three sheets in the wind**. In that case, what you'll need the morning after is another alcoholic drink to revive you, idiomatically known as (and here comes that doggie again!) a **hair of the dog**.

A hangover isn't usually fatal though, even if you're feeling that you might be **on your last legs**. If you want to talk about dying, then someone who dies is said to **kick the bucket**, **drop off the twig**, **bite the dust**, **peg out**, **cash in their chips**, or **pop their clogs**. Doesn't sound so bad when you can dress it up as a colourful idiom, does it? But that's not much consolation when you're **pushing up the daisies**!

But there's no need to dwell on such gloomy matters. Let's hope you're **in the pink** (perfectly healthy). You might have been **born with a silver spoon in your mouth** (born into a wealthy family), in which case you can lead **the life of Riley**. If you're used to getting **the full monty** in everything, then don't be surprised if less fortunate people envy you. They'd be **over the moon** if they had your advantages. But they can always console themselves with whatever they've got and decide that it's **better than a poke in the eye with a dry stick**.

You might be happy now, but soon you could be **laughing on the other side of your face**. If something about your situation is not to your liking, it's better to be completely frank and **make no bones about it**. It's pointless to **beat about the bush** if you've **had it up to here** (have had more than enough). Is work getting you down? Maybe a disgruntled boss has **come down on you like a ton of bricks**, even though you've been **minding your p's and q's** and working hard **like nobody's business**. When it looks like they've **got it in for you** and **the writing's on the wall** (things look as if they're coming to an end) as far as your job is concerned, try not to **lose your bottle** (run out of courage). Perhaps they're imposing wage cuts **across the board**. Nobody can say you don't know when you're not wanted – after all, you're **not wet behind the ears**. Maybe you already had **ants in your pants** and were up for a new challenge. Ready to give up the struggle? Why not **call it a day**?

Many familiar idioms have origins that are by no means obvious to a modern speaker. The expression **between the devil and the deep blue sea**, for example, is actually a nautical reference rather than the formulation of a choice between going to hell and drowning. The 'devil' in question, was the seam on a sailing ship where the deck joined the side. A sailor who was precariously suspended on a rope beyond this seam, to perform some act of maintenance, might therefore be described as being between the devil and the deep blue sea. The idiom **the devil to pay** also refers to this seam: the original expression was 'the devil to pay and no pitch hot', referring to the troublesome situation of being required to pay the seam (that is, paint it with tar) without adequate equipment.

WHAT THE HECK?

The British have always been good at **euphemisms**. What is a euphemism? It's when you substitute a milder expression for the one you first thought of, which seems as if it might be a little too offensive or upsetting. Maybe our fondness for this type of expression has something to do with the national characteristic of not wanting to cause any trouble or annoy anyone – although other nations might say we're just too inhibited!

The areas in which this kind of watering down of language goes on are pretty obvious when you think about it. What things do we most dislike talking plainly about? Why sex, bodily functions, death, and bad language of course!

Those who are old enough presumably know what is involved in sexual intercourse, but how often do we hear that someone has **slept with** someone else, when it's clear that no actual sleeping has taken place? What, in an aeroplane toilet? Don't think so! And if this activity should result in a pregnancy, do we come right out and say so? No, we talk about the woman as being **in the family way**, or if (heavens forfend!) there is scandal attached, **in trouble**. At least we have left behind the favourite Victorian expression which had it that the woman was **in an interesting condition**.

We describe films, books, or other forms of entertainment that have a sexual content as being **adult**, even when their content is pitched at the most immature of adolescent levels. And when a female performer's act consists principally of taking off her clothes in a provocative manner we call her an **exotic dancer**.

You might need to go to the toilet, but you can't just blurt out its name! No, you talk about going to the **loo** or the **bathroom** (though you probably don't intend to have a bath), or if you want to be even more precious about it, the **ladies' room** or the **little boys' room**. Some people still say they have to **spend a penny**, even though the days of public toilets operated by a penny coin are long gone. You can't discuss what goes on there, of course, but if pressed, perhaps by your doctor, you might reach back to childhood and admit to performing a **number one** or **number two**. As for toilet paper, don't be coarse! Say **bathroom tissue** or, if you're being informal, **loo roll**.

The British expression **under the weather** is what we say we are when we're ill, and this can cover everything from a slight cold to a much more serious condition. If you're in such a bad way that you actually, not to put too fine a point on it, die, then you're said to have **passed**. This is rather unimaginative compared to such euphemisms of the past as having **joined the choir invisible** or being **asleep in the bosom of Abraham**. This idea of death as a form of slumber is also applied to animals when we talk about having our pets **put to sleep**. You might want Towser to be **put out of his misery**, but maybe he'd rather be miserable than dead!

Some words and expressions are still considered taboo in everyday language, although these grow fewer every day, and the most explicit of **effing and blinding** may be heard on television or in films. Even the word 'language' itself has become a euphemism for swearing. Look at your latest DVD box: does it warn you that it contains 'mild language'? **What the dickens** does that mean? Do the characters say things like **cripes**, **gee whizz**, **dash it all**, or some **blooming** thing like that? What's the world coming to, **for Pete's sake**?

> The word 'euphemism' comes from two Greek words:
> *eu* meaning 'well' and *pheme* meaning 'speech'. So a euphemism
> is a 'good speech' even if it refers to something regarded as
> bad or shameful.

NOW THERE'S A FUNNY THING

The British are renowned for their **sense of humour**. This may be partly because we find it easier to bear the troubles of life by putting a humorous spin on them, and partly because the English language has a rich and varied vocabulary that lends itself easily to wordplay. In this section we look at what tickles the nation's funny bone and pay tribute to its greatest wits.

In the eighteenth century **Samuel Johnson** established himself as one of the nation's greatest conversationalists and was rarely at a loss for a quip. Typical Johnsonian utterances include, 'Sir, a woman's preaching is like a dog's walking on his hinder legs. It is not done well; but you are surprised to find it done at all.'

In the following century, **Oscar Wilde** proved himself the master of the witty retort. Speaking to a customs official on entering America he stated, 'I have nothing to declare except my genius', and even lying on his deathbed in Paris he had the presence of mind to remark, 'Either that wallpaper goes, or I do.'

Wilde's fellow-Irishman **George Bernard Shaw** was another writer with a gift for making clever remarks. He declared that 'If all economists were laid end to end, they would not reach a conclusion', and turning to another profession described a drama critic as someone who 'leaves no turn unstoned'. It's no surprise that he also remarked, 'I often quote myself. It adds spice to the conversation.'

Among the humorists to emerge after the Second World War the most original was probably **Spike Milligan**, who created a new brand of zany humour in *The Goon Show*. Milligan famously quipped that his tombstone should bear the words, 'I told you I was ill.'

The 1960s saw a boom in satire as *That Was The Week That Was* and *Beyond the Fringe* delighted in taking swipes at the establishment. **Peter Cook** typified this new irreverence by portraying Prime

Minister Harold Macmillan returning from a summit in America: 'We talked of many things, including Great Britain's position in the world as some kind of honest broker. I agreed with him when he said no nation could be more honest, and he agreed with me when I chaffed him and said no nation could be broker.'

By the end of the decade *Monty Python*'s surreal humour held sway. This comedy was often visual or depended on absurd situations, and although many lines from Python are frequently quoted, you really need to have seen the original sketches to know why saying 'This is an ex-parrot' or 'No-one expects the Spanish Inquisition' should reduce roomfuls of Brits to helpless giggles.

Although writers and comedians continue to amuse, it is now often advertisers and newspaper sub-editors who make the most creative use of wordplay. Take the shop selling camping equipment who paraphrased a famous line of Shakespeare to announce, 'Now is the discount of our winter tents'.

In particular, tabloid newspapers such as *The Sun* make an art form of finding punning or allusive headlines to capture the leading story of the day. An attempted diamond robbery at the Millennium Dome prompted the headline 'I'm Only Here For De Beers' – an allusion to a famous commercial – while a defeat for the English football team against Sweden saw the national manager portrayed as a vegetable while *The Sun* exclaimed, 'Swedes 2, Turnips 1'. Another typical headline of a more recent vintage relates to the supposed frustration expressed by French politician Nicolas Sarkozy at press intrusion into the private affairs of his wife Carla Bruni: 'Sarky Gets Narky at Carla Malarky'.

YOU ARE AWFUL ...
BUT I LIKE YOU!

The British love their **catchphrases** and frequently drop them into their everyday conversation on the assumption that the people they are talking to will get the reference to a favourite entertainer or show.

People remember these catchphrases because they hear them so often, but why do they repeat them at every opportunity? It's got a lot to do with solidarity: if you know the same catchphrases as someone else it's easier to establish common ground or fit into a group, especially if the phrases in question are 'owned' by an exclusive set of people. It's also a shorthand way of showing that you're a fun person, that you like a laugh, and have a good sense of humour. If you don't know the latest, most fashionable catchphrases you'll seem hopelessly 'out of the loop' and what's more, you'll probably be totally mystified by the references that are being bandied about all around you.

The first true catchphrases were those that were identified with popular comedians or variety entertainers. There are exceptions, of course. Think of the immortal private detective Sherlock Holmes, and certain words immediately spring to mind: **elementary, my dear Watson**. (It doesn't matter that his creator Arthur Conan Doyle never actually wrote such a phrase, and that it probably first appeared much later in a film script.)

What we often forget is that before television came along performances were live, and the performers would make a living by constantly touring theatres up and down the country. Each 'gig' would be a one-night stand, so there was no pressing need to have new material for every performance and each entertainer would hone their act until it was as good as they could make it. They soon discovered which of their gag lines went down best and would repeat them at every opportunity. This is how a veteran entertainer like Bruce Forsyth came up with his catchphrase **nice to see you, to see you ... nice**!

The same was true of comedians like Frank Carson (**it's the way I tell 'em!**) and Larry Grayson (**shut that door!** or **look at the muck on here!**). The duo Morecambe and Wise famously had a two-part, question and answer catchphrase that they would throw in at some point in every show: **What do you think of it so far? Rubbish!** They say that television killed the live variety show, but many performers survived the demise of variety and successfully transferred their acts to the new medium, whether as performers in the same old way or as hosts of game shows or chat shows.

We shouldn't forget the part played by radio, which was the most widespread broadcast medium before television superseded it. Regular programmes like *ITMA* (It's That Man Again) gave the nation such catchphrases as:

- ❖ **Can I do you now, sir?**

- ❖ **I go, I come back**

- ❖ **TTFN** (ta-ta for now)

Another programme that had a cult following (which famously included Prince Charles) was *The Goon Show*, with its collection of zany character like Eccles, Neddy Seagoon, and Bluebottle, who unfailingly regularly delivered lines like:

- ❖ **You rotten swine!**

- ❖ **You silly, twisted boy!**

- ❖ **He's fallen in the water!**

- ❖ **Ying Tong Iddle-I Po**

Comedy has always been big on TV, not just in the form of stand-up comedians telling jokes, but more importantly for the spread of catchphrases, in long-running sketch shows or sitcoms.

Monty Python's Flying Circus was a surrealistic sketch show that branded many catchphrases on to the national consciousness. A sudden transition from one seemingly unfinished sketch to another would be announced by '**And now for something completely different**'. If a protesting character foolishly uttered the line 'I didn't expect the Spanish Inquisition' this was a cue for the appearance of characters dressed in the robes and crucifixes of just such Inquisitors, one of whom would inevitably declaim, '**Nobody expects the Spanish Inquisition!**' The famous 'Dead Parrot' sketch yielded the phrase **this is an ex-parrot**, which was much copied and adapted (dare we say 'parroted'?), and the intellectually-challenged 'Gumby' characters came up with **my brain hurts**. This was perhaps the first show from which its geekiest devotees could recite whole sketches, not just catchphrases!

Other sketch shows followed, which generated their own memorable lines, including *The Fast Show*, with **I was very, very drunk**, **suit you, sir!**, **Scorchio!**, **I'll get me coat**, ... and **which was nice**. *Little Britain* exposed the nation to **the only gay in the village**, **computer says no**, ... and **I want that one**, while *The Catherine Tate Show* spawned **How very dare you!** and most memorably made it into the *Oxford English Dictionary* with **Am I bovvered?** *The Mighty Boosh* contributed **I got a bad feeling about this**, which can be, and is, trotted out on all sorts of occasions!

British television sitcoms have always been a fertile source of catchphrases. Appearing in a regular time slot (at least before the advent of multi-channel TV), if they were well written they would garner a loyal audience. One of the most long-running was *Dad's Army*, which popularized such phrase as:

- ❖ **Stupid boy!**
- ❖ **Don't panic!**
- ❖ **We're doomed!**
- ❖ **They don't like it up 'em!**

I'm free! was the regular utterance of Mr Humphreys, a somewhat effeminate character in *Are You Being Served?* as he put himself forward for any task. In *The Fall and Rise of Reginald Perrin* the overbearing boss, CJ, invariably boasted of his own business prowess in pompous lines inevitably beginning with **I didn't get where I am today…**, while another, ex-military character was always lamenting **a bit of a cock-up on the catering front**.

Only Fools and Horses was a favourite for many years and had everybody repeating its recurrent phrases like **lovely jubbly**, **you plonker**, and **cushty!** The character Victor Meldrew in *One Foot in the Grave* frequently responded to his latest setback with **I don't believe it!** So popular was this curmudgeonly, always disappointed, personage that his very name became a catchphrase itself, applied to any grumpy old man.

On television there's always been a connection between comedy and game shows, with famous comedians taking their turn as hosts and making good use of their own catchphrases. In fact, there was even a game show called *Catchphrase* in which contestants had to identify idioms from visual clues, thus giving its host, Roy Walker, his memorable line **say what you see**. In *The Generation Game* Bruce Forsyth's regular comments included **good game, good game**, **didn't he** (or **she**) **do well?** and **give us a twirl** (when asking the show's hostess to show off her latest extravagant gown). When the eventual winner had to remember what prizes had flitted past on a conveyor belt, members of the audience would invariably call out **cuddly toy!**

Other game-show catchphrases include Magnus Magnusson's magisterial insistence on completing a question (**I've started, so I'll finish**), *The Weakest Link*'s **you *are* the weakest link!** and the host Chris Tarrant's temporizing question **final answer?** in *Who Wants to be a Millionaire?*

IT'S GOOD TO TALK

As is true of most countries, Britain is awash with **advertising**. On television, the advertising breaks seem to drag on so long that we are in danger of losing the thread of what we were watching. The internet, radio, and cinema also do their share while our towns and cities are wallpapered with billboards and posters. Hardly a vehicle (or increasingly even a person!) passes in the street without an advertising slogan on unashamed display. Is it any wonder, then, that advertising slogans can become fixed in people's consciousness?

It doesn't so much matter what the rest of an advert consists of as long as it ends with a memorable catchphrase. Just like the hook to a catchy song, a well-crafted slogan will stick in your mind whether you want it to or not, and over the years many have become so familiar that people use them in everyday conversation. Sometimes they make for a shared joke; often quoting them just shows that you are hip to the latest trends.

Brits enjoy their beer, as every adman worth his salt knows, often to the extent of being (as one campaign phrased it) **only here for the beer**. Of course, while people are always on the lookout for bargains in booze, nobody wants to be associated with low-end products, and that's why purveyors of beer tell you that their particular brew is **reassuringly expensive** or **probably** (how modest!) **the best lager in the world**. Others claim to have special qualities that no competitor could possibly match, such as being **good for you**, being able to **work wonders**, or to **refresh the parts that other beers cannot reach**. As you see, a little innuendo never goes astray when appealing to those who like a drink! It's enough to make you switch to something soft and fizzy, as long as it's **the real thing**! Or better yet, being British, stick to **tea you can really taste**.

Supermarkets are always at the cutting edge of deadly price wars, and their slogans tend to reflect the importance of value for money for every product. That's why one tells us that

every little helps, while another will offer **more reasons** to shop there or **everything you want from a store and a little bit more**. One major chain promises that they can help you **live well for less**, and yet another asserts that it has its own price, driving home the message with an accompanying slap (self-administered of course!) on an actor's bottom.

Car manufacturers get in on the act by offering not just a runaround to take you to the shops but a whole glamorous lifestyle. One claims that their products have **va va voom**, while not making it exactly clear what that is (sounds foreign, so it must be good!) while a competitor has managed to get us all repeating a phrase in another language that means little to most punters but does sound terribly impressive: **vorsprung durch technik**, anyone? Unless you're bilingual, you couldn't claim in this case, unlike a certain brand of varnish, that it's a case of **exactly what it says on the tin**!

A bit of flattery goes a long way too, and millions of British ladies have been convinced that they're **worth it** simply because a manufacturer of cosmetics takes the time to tell them so. And what self-respecting male wouldn't want to make sure he shaves with **the best a man can get**?

Whatever we feel moved to lavish our cash on, cost won't matter when we're all millionaires. As the National Lottery adverts tell us, **it could be you**!

The magazine *Marketing* holds an annual poll to decide the most irritating advertising campaign broadcast on British television. In both 2010 and 2011 the award was won by the price-comparison website Go Compare, whose adverts feature a Welsh tenor belting out the name of the company in various improbable settings.

DON'T CALL ME
A CHAV, INNIT?

Slang is the kind of language they don't teach you at school. It's too informal to be neatly categorized and broken down into easily learnable bits, and it's often too rude to be admitted into any respectable curriculum. The British Isles are home to all sorts of slang: some kinds belong to particular groups in society; some are found only in certain parts of the country; still others are typical of individual trades or professions. And they're usually not mutually understandable! Here we take a shufti at some of the varieties of slang to be found in the United Kingdom.

There's no doubt that the most colourful and inventive slang comes from the streets of our larger cities and it's the young (the **yoof**) who are coining and circulating it. If you like to enjoy yourself enthusiastically you might say you want to **large it** by going out **on the razz**, maybe in the process getting **off your face** (intoxicated), and always in the hope of meeting some attractive members of the opposite sex (**copping off** with some **totty** or **talent**). On the other hand, you might prefer to **take a chill pill** and relax while listening to a few **tunes**. Anything you disapprove of can be described as **gay** (with no offence meant towards homosexuals), while an unattractive person can be dismissed as a **minger** or a **munter**.

Much of the slang generated by the hip-hop culture owes its origin to the United States, but kids who are into it in Britain are equally au fait with the vocabulary:

bling	showy jewellery or clothes
booty	the buttocks
def	excellent
fly	fashionable or stylish
massive	a gang or just a group of friends
props	respect (as in 'give someone their props')

DON'T CALL ME A CHAV, INNIT?

At the other end of the social scale from street culture is the social group who were known in the 1980s as Sloane Rangers, easily identified by their signature phrase **OK yah**! These young people are rich and well-connected, and although they may not call themselves Sloanes any more they still have their own slang terms such as **disrevelled** (how you look the morning after a night on the tiles), **squippy** (full of enthusiasm), **birdage** (a collective term for attractive young women), **jollop** (to enjoy oneself at a party or other social event – which in the circles they move in will probably be **GLO** or guest list only), and **floordrobe** (the floor as a resting place for one's range of clothes when not in use).

Britain in the twenty-first century is nothing if not multicultural and British slang certainly reflects this. The influence of people of Afro-Caribbean ethnic background is so prevalent in some circles, especially in Greater London, that a kind of hybrid slang called **Jafaikan** has been identified.

Or perhaps you speak **Hinglish**? The influence of the languages of the Indian subcontinent such as Hindi, Punjabi, and Urdu has also become more strongly defined among British Asians. Most of us have long been familiar with the menu items of Asian cuisine, but how many would readily understand the Hinglish words below?

airdash	a great hurry
badmash	a hooligan or criminal
chuddies	underpants
glassy	thirsty
timepass	a hobby or pastime

DASH IT ALL!

We all know what **swearing** is, even if we are too polite to resort to it ourselves, and we all know the basic words that are most commonly used, especially 'the f-word' and 'the c-word'. Sex and sexuality, body parts and functions, and matters of race and religion have always generated terms of abuse and offensive language. Whatever you call them ... Anglo-Saxon, four-letter words, foul language ... we don't have to spell them out here. And, of course, spelling them out is exactly what many publications *don't* do! How often, especially in newspapers, do we see lines of asterisks appearing after an initial F or C? In fact, one of the most popular euphemisms for proper swearing, **dash**, came into use because of the printers' practice of indicating taboo words with a dash.

What is considered taboo language in one generation may become generally acceptable in another. Take '**damn**' for example, when used as a swearword. Victorian printers would never have shown this in full, giving us 'd—' at the most, and writers would get round it by using a euphemism like 'dash' or 'darn'. But certainly by the mid-twentieth century not very many people would take offence at seeing it in print. After Clark Gable had delivered his famous final line in the 1939 movie *Gone With The Wind* ('Frankly, my dear, I don't give a damn!') that particular genie was not going back into the bottle.

Similarly, the exclamation '**Oh, my God!**' would have been regarded as shocking as late as the early twentieth century. After all, it's an example of something expressly forbidden by the Christian Bible, taking the Lord's name in vain. However, by the end of that century it had become an automatic phrase that people, even children, blithely used to react to any surprise, however minor.

In racial abuse, what we can refer to here as 'the N-word' for a black person has long been considered too offensive for unrestricted use. Yet, when black people themselves began to use the word as a term of address for one another, almost as a badge of belonging, it gained a new lease of life. The word 'queer' when used as a derogatory term for a homosexual underwent a comparable process, emerging as a positive label when used by gay people, to the extent that it is perfectly acceptable to talk about 'queer cinema'.

'**Bastard**' used to be one of the vilest insults that could be thrown at a man. It suggested, of course, that the person in question was of illegitimate birth, born to parents who weren't married. Nowadays, with the increasing decline of formal marriage in Britain, the idea of being 'born out of wedlock' is not only perfectly acceptable but is so common as to pass without comment. How we used to struggle to suppress our giggles at metalwork class in school when the teacher described a particular file as being 'bastard cut'! All he meant what that its teeth were intermediate between a coarse cut and a fine cut. Now a 'bastard' can be anything we dislike, from a difficult job to a painful headache, or even a general term for a person ('Poor old bastard!').

One of the commonest British expletives (a fancy term for a word that adds force to a statement without adding any meaning) is **bloody**, and you would have to be a pretty stern moralist to object to its use these days. However, did you know that some people reckon it's a garbled form of 'by Our Lady', a form of swearing by the Virgin Mary that once would have been considered blasphemous?

A LITTLE BIRD
TOLD ME

When mobile phones first became widely available in Britain in the late twentieth century, it wasn't just the ability to speak to each other anytime anywhere that was unleashed on the airwaves. In no time at all the ability of SMS services to send text messages became as important as the ability to make and receive calls. Not only is texting more private than talking, it is also more succinct. As an incidental effect it introduced a new verb to the English language – I text, you text, we texted – created from a word that for centuries had been content to do duty as a noun.

Text messaging quickly evolved a language of its own (**textspeak**) which makes extensive use of abbreviations:

LOL	lots of love or laughing out loud
ROTFL	rolling on the floor laughing
IMHO	in my humble opinion
FYI	for your information
BBFN	bye-bye for now
BTW	by the way

Numbers were also brought in to communicate the sounds of words, as in:

L8R	later	**2NITE**	tonight
H8	hate	**4EVER**	forever
2DAY	today	**GR8**	great

You could even convey a state of mind by means of symbols called **smileys** or **emoticons**. These are basically clever uses of existing punctuation marks already available on any keyboard, with the understanding that they should be read 'on their side'. The most popular examples are:

:)	happy
: (	sad
: **D**	laughing
;)	winking

Communications technology never stands still for long in the twenty-first century. Mobile phones soon evolved into 'smartphones' with capabilities and applications (henceforth known to the cognoscenti as **apps**) undreamt of by Alexander Graham Bell or even the writers of *Star Trek*. Indeed devices like the Blackberry seem to be able to do everything except beam you up! People use them not only to communicate, and to organize their lives but to document them in their blogs or **moblogs**.

Social networking websites like Facebook were the next step. These allowed entire 'virtual' communities to be established online, with subscribers being enabled to interact without ever having to endure the inconvenience of meeting face to face (or **F2F** in textspeak). It was in 2006 that one of these, Twitter, gave us another new meaning for an old word. Suddenly to **tweet** meant not to sing like a little bird but to post a message (also called **a tweet**) on the Twitter site. The fact that these tweets are limited in extent to 140 words means that the abbreviations already in common use in text messaging are ideal. You might think that this restriction would discourage waffling, but it's probably truer to say that the net result is that there's still as much inconsequentiality and nonsense – it's just more succinctly expressed!

Twitter's popularity also established some of its own language uses in the everyday vocabulary of the general public. You might never have tweeted yourself, but you will possibly be familiar with such terms as **follow**, **hashtag**, **retweet**, and **trending topic**. It's even possible for Twitter devotees (the **Twitterati**) to actually come together at specially organized events known as **Tweetups**.

OUT WITH
THE OLD ...

The English language has never stood still. It is always changing as new words and expressions are invented and become more widely used, while existing words may develop new uses or nuances or gradually discard their original meaning altogether. Here we look at some words that have fallen out of general use. It's interesting, though, how far words that are now old-fashioned or even obsolete refuse to disappear entirely and can still be come across – and not just in the pages of a dictionary!

Changes in grammar can account for lots of words dropping out of use. Nowhere outside the plays of Shakespeare or his contemporaries or other forms of historical literature will you encounter words like **didst**, **dost**, **doth**, **hadst**, **hast**, **hath**, **mayst**, **saith**, **sayest**, **shouldst**, **wert**, or **wouldst**. In English, unlike many other modern languages, we have lost the distinction between formal and informal ways of addressing people, which means we always say 'you' and never bother with **thee** and **thou**.

Probably the biggest category of obsolete terms contains words that became redundant because they referred to things that have ceased to exist. Here are a few examples:

changeling a child supposedly stolen by fairies

dandiprat a small sixteenth-century English coin

galliard a spirited dance of the sixteenth and seventeenth centuries

gyves chains fastened on a prisoner's ankles

handsel a gift given at New Year for good luck

scrivener a person who makes handwritten copies of documents

scullion a servant who does rough menial work

seneschal the steward of a medieval nobleman

whiffler an attendant who clears the way for a procession

Other words simply get replaced by newer terms for the same thing, sometimes when a little updating is needed, but often because people prefer to use something that is less of a mouthful. You can see probably see why some of the following fell out of use!

bezonian a rascal or dishonest person

caitiff a coward

clapperclaw to scratch with the fingernails

cordwainer a shoemaker

draggletailed dirty or untidy

drysalter a shopkeeper who sells mostly dried goods

empyrean the heavens or sky

fabricant a manufacturer

fardel something that you carry; a burden

foeman an enemy

footpad a highwayman who robs you on foot – a mugger

fustigate to beat someone, especially using a cudgel

hoodman-blind the game of blind man's buff

izzard the letter Z

mafficking extravagant and public celebration

mansuetude gentleness or mildness

mooncalf a silly or stupid person

obmutescence persistent silence ('I'm saying nothing!')

orgulous proud

paranymph a bridesmaid or best man

pesthouse a hospital for infectious diseases

pilgarlic a bald man

slubberdegullion a slovenly person

vaunt-courier a forerunner

whim-wham a fancy thing of no great value

> **wittol** a man who knows his wife is unfaithful but who puts up with it
>
> **yclept** known by the name of; 'called', in other words

The creation and use of insults is always a fertile field of language, but even the worst of these that you can fling at one another lose their force over time. You've got to keep up to date if you want to slag someone off effectively, so nowadays it's no use calling a woman of loose morals a **Cyprian**, **doxy**, **drab**, **quean**, **strumpet**, or **trull**. Best stick to 'ho' if you really must be so unpleasant. Similarly, you'll be wasting your time if think a male you dislike will be fazed by being tagged as a **dastard**, a **hobbledehoy**, **jackanapes**, **losel**, **rakehell**, **recreant**, **runagate**, **varlet**, **whoremaster**, or **whoreson**.

In recent times the all-purpose exclamation 'Oh, my God!' has come to be used on all possible occasions, covering everything from mild surprise to a shock of heart-attack-inducing proportions. In the past we were more inventive and were able to call on a wider stock of verbal reactions, such as **alack** (or **alackaday**, to be more elaborate), **begad**, **egad**, **fie**, **gadzooks**, **lackaday**, **lawks**, **marry** (a reference to the Virgin Mary, not to an impulsive expression of desire to be wed!), **swounds**, **wellaway**, and **zounds**.

Then there are words that have almost completely died out in their original form but which persist in everyday language as part of compound terms or expressions. No-one nowadays would use **feck** to mean 'worth or value' (the Irish, of course would use it rather differently!) but we all know what 'feckless' means. In the same way, we can all be ruthless if we must, but none of us would recognize feeling **ruth** (meaning 'compassion, pity, or remorse'). **Mere**, the old word for a lake is seldom heard now except as part of proper names like Windermere or Grasmere; nor is **hurst** a

wood or a sandbank, much used other than in placenames like Billingshurst or Wadhurst.

Finally, when you're reading English literature of past centuries you've got to be careful not to assume that you know the meaning of a word just because it looks familiar. Words that are spelled the same haven't always meant the same thing. To round off our rummage through the lost-property box of the English language, here are some examples of words that you probably think you know but which have been used with an altogether different meaning in the past:

fell cruel or fierce (as in 'one fell swoop')

goody a married woman of low rank

list to desire or please

natural an imbecile or idiot

neat a cow

nice foolish or ignorant

pard not a cowboy's friend but a leopard or panther

puissance power

sack white wine

weird your fate or destiny

... IN WITH THE NEW

As some old words disappear from the language, they are more than compensated for by the number of new words coming into it. These may describe new developments in society or technology – things that didn't exist before and so need a name. In recent years we have all become used to hearing about **blogs**, **podcasts**, and **tweets**, and yet none of these words – or concepts – existed before the twenty-first century. But even without this stimulus there is still a perpetual desire to describe existing things in fresh and interesting ways and this also helps to swell the pages of the dictionary.

New words may be formed by borrowing words from other languages or by fusing together two existing words or parts of existing words. Or they may be taken from the initial letters of a phrase (these are called 'acronyms') or by using the name of a person associated with a thing. Here is a selection of words that have recently been spotted in English for the first time. Many will undoubtedly fall away into obscurity as the things they describe turn out to be of only temporary interest, whereas others will take root and establish themselves as permanent fixtures in the English lexicon.

alpha mummy a woman who excels in the art of motherhood

amortal a person who refuses to acknowledge the processes of ageing and mortality

Arab Spring a period in which Arab people seek democratic reforms

babycino a drink of frothy milk with a chocolate topping, designed as an alternative to coffee for young children

Big Society the devolution of political power and social responsibility to local communities as opposed to centralized political power and state control

casino banking an approach to banking which risks losing investors' money in the quest for maximizing profits

cellfish using a mobile phone in a way that disregards the wishes of other people

clickjacking the practice of using a disguised hyperlink to direct an internet user to a website he or she does not wish to visit

clicktivism a policy of using the internet to take direct and often militant action to achieve a political or social aim

ecotarian a person who eats only food that has been produced in an environmentally-friendly manner

fanpire an ardent admirer of films and television programmes that feature vampires

fauxminist a person who makes an insincere pretence of feminism

foodoir a book or blog that combines a personal memoir with a series of recipes

frape to alter information in a person's profile on a social networking website without his or her permission

funemployment the condition of a person who enjoys being out of work

gender disappointment a feeling of depression or anxiety experienced by an expectant parent when the gender of the baby does not match his or her preference

ghost estate a housing estate built during an economic boom but unfinished or unoccupied during a recession

hashtag a tag consisting of the symbol # followed by a word or series of concatenated words, used on social networking sites to enable users to find trending topics of interest

haul queen a young woman who displays her recent shopping purchases in films uploaded to video-sharing websites, and is paid according to the advertising revenue those videos generate

intexticated (said of a driver) distracted while writing or reading a text message on a mobile phone

jeggings women's leggings designed to look like tight denim jeans

livestream to broadcast an event on the internet as it happens

manband an all-male vocal pop group which was formed as a boy band, but whose members have reached maturity

mankini a man's swimming costume consisting of a narrow V-shaped piece of material extending from the crotch to the shoulders

mumpreneur a woman who combines running a business enterprise with looking after her children

murderabilia objects that are regarded as valuable because of their connection with murders or other notorious crimes

PIIGS Portugal, Italy, Ireland, Greece, and Spain, seen collectively as the members of the European single currency whose national economies are least stable

quantitative easing the practice of increasing the supply of money in order to stimulate economic activity

randomer an unspecified person of no importance

schooligan a person of school age who engages in acts of public disorder

sexting the practice of sending sexually explicit text messages

SMiShing the practice of using fraudulent text messages to extract financial data from users for purposes of identity theft

traffic-light labelling a system of food labelling in which red, amber, and green symbols are used to indicate whether the food contains high, medium, or low amounts of sugar, fat, salt, etc

unicorn chaser a comforting or innocent image, video clip, or topic viewed or contemplated following a previous, disturbing image, video, etc (originally a picture of a unicorn posted on a blog site shortly after an offensive or disturbing picture has been posted, as a kind of antidote to the previous post)

vertical farming a proposed system of growing crops in urban areas using specially designed skyscrapers

warbot any robot or unmanned vehicle or device designed for and used in warfare

warmist a person, especially a scientist, who believes in global warming and the greenhouse effect (as opposed to a **coolist**)

weapon dog a dog, especially a bulldog or pit bull terrier, kept as a pet and trained to intimidate and attack others

wikiality a version of facts which is agreed to be true, but which may not coincide with objective reality

A TOUR

of

BRITAIN

A DISUNITED KINGDOM?

The twenty-first century promises to be a challenging period for the United Kingdom. In 1997 a separate Scottish parliament was established while a national assembly was set up for Wales, and an assembly for Northern Ireland followed in 1998. The idea may have been to give the nations a degree of autonomy while keeping them within the United Kingdom. However, the increasing unpopularity of the major national political parties has seen a corresponding growth in support for independence in Scotland, and a referendum is set to take place to decide this issue in 2014.

Whether or not the Scottish people vote to become a separate nation, the campaign for independence reminds us that Britain is by no means a uniform country. It is formed from peoples who once spoken different languages and spent hundreds of years fighting against each other. People can still be fiercely proud of their home patch. Moreover, it is not just the Scots, Welsh, and Northern Irish who are keen to distance themselves from the English. In places such as Cornwall and Yorkshire, too, pride in one's county may outweigh pride in one's country. The truth is that most of us are a little bit ambivalent when it comes to our national identity: at times we think of ourselves as British, and at other times we identify with our local area or nation.

In the final part of the book we take a tour around the different regions that make up the United Kingdom. The American writer Bill Bryson observed that 'nowhere, of course, are the British more gifted than with place names', and we drop in on some of the more quirkily-named spots on the map of Britain, as well as looking at some of the informal names adopted by our towns and cities.

However, the main theme of our final section is on the different versions of English that are spoken around the British Isles. We start in the capital city London and consider the dialect that can be heard there, learning a few words of its famous Cockney rhyming slang. From there, we head to the principality of Wales, where the Welsh language is still very much alive and has affected the local form of English both in terms of vocabulary and the typical patterns of speech. In Scotland, the way that English is spoken is the product of a collision between Anglo-Saxon and the Gaelic language, but we also find distinctive variations, with the west, the east, and the north-east of the country all having their own dialects. The English spoken in Northern Ireland is also a fusion of Anglo-Saxon and Gaelic, and here more than anywhere the history of the language reflects the political history of the province.

We end our tour by calling in on some of the regions of England. There has been definite shift away from dialect toward a more standardized form of English in recent years as we are now more geographically mobile and we all watch the same films and television programmes. Nevertheless, there are still many variations in the English you will hear as you travel around these islands, and we provide some glossaries to give a flavour of some of the different dialects.

When we look at the dialects spoken around Britain we can see many differences in the way that English is spoken. Yet there are also some interesting similarities. For example, the Scottish word 'stravaig' pops up in the Midlands as 'strayve', while the Welsh word 'cwm' is found in the West Country as 'coomb'. Perhaps we have more in common that we thought.

PLACES WITH STRANGE-SOUNDING NAMES

Because so many different peoples have layered their languages onto the fabric of these islands – Celts, Picts, Romans, Vikings, Angles, Saxons, Normans, and so on – looking at a map of Britain can reveal the history of our nation through the names of its towns, cities, and villages. Some of the names are as picturesque and charming as the places themselves – or even more so! Here are some of our favourites:

❖ There are two places in England called **Beer**, one a village in Devon and the other a hamlet in Somerset, which is across a river from the site of a medieval village called **Oath**. Surprisingly, Beer does not come from the drink, but from an Anglo-Saxon word meaning 'grove'.

❖ The Scottish village of **Lost** has an unfortunate experience of regularly having the road signs to it stolen, leading many people travelling there to become, well, lost.

❖ In North Norfolk there are two beautiful, sleepy villages called **Great Snoring** and **Little Snoring**. In the Domesday Book the place is listed as 'Snaringa', which means someone called Snear once lived there.

❖ **Scratchy Bottom** lies near to the rather wonderfully named **Durdle Door**, a huge limestone arch stretching out into the sea in Dorset. Scratchy Bottom is a dry valley which can't be farmed, and as such the floor of the valley is a little rough...

❖ In Staffordshire there is an oddly-named village called **Weston-under-Lizard**. Luckily the Lizard in this case is the name of a hill overlooking the village, and does not indicate the site of a Godzilla-type disaster.

❖ **Westward Ho!** is the only British place name to include an exclamation mark. It was named after a novel by the Victorian writer Charles Kingsley, in the hope that this would induce more people to go there on holiday. The only other place in the world with an exclamation mark is Saint-Louis-du-Ha! Ha! in Quebec.

❖ There are many theories as to why **Pity Me**, near Durham, is so named. The strongest theory at the moment is that it is named after the desolate nature and poor-quality soil of the surroundings.

❖ Rather more cheerful-sounding than Pity Me, **Giggleswick**, a village in Yorkshire, is so named because there was a farm (possibly a dairy) there belonging to a farmer named Gikel. This is frankly a little disappointing, but we are sure that there is plenty there to amuse you should you visit.

❖ **Hill O Many Stanes** is a place that says it like it is – a hillside in Caithness in the north of Scotland that is covered with nearly two hundred short standing 'stanes' (the Scots word for stones). We don't know why they were put there, or what they were for, but someone in the Bronze Age must have had a plan.

❖ Last, and certainly not least, we come to **Llanfairpwllgwyngyllgogerychwyrndrobwllllantysilio-gogogoch**. This village on the Welsh island of Anglesey has the distinction of being the longest place name in Britain, and roughly means 'St. Mary's Church (Llanfair) in the hollow (pwll) of the white hazel (gwyngyll) near (goger) the rapid whirlpool (y chwyrndrobwll) and the church of St. Tysilio (llantysilio) with a red cave (gogogoch)'. Phew!

DO YOU KNOW THE WAY TO SILICON FEN?

Besides the names by which they are formally known, and which you will see on maps and road signs, some British places have also acquired nicknames. These may even be embraced by the local authorities and used to attract visitors to the area – although not all of them are complimentary!

Some places are associated with a particular industry, such as the area around Stoke-on-Trent that is called **the Potteries** because of its role as a centre of the ceramics trade. For the same reason, Sheffield is known as **the Steel City**, while the heavily industrialized area around Wolverhampton is called **the Black Country** in reference to the colour of the smoke emanating from its factory chimneys.

It has been noted earlier in this book that smoke is a common theme in city nicknames, reflecting the time when the burning of fuels had a pervasive effect on the urban environment. London is still known **the Big Smoke** (or often simply **the Smoke**), while the Scottish capital Edinburgh is called **Auld Reekie** (a Scots phrase meaning 'Old Smoky'). Yet 'the Smoke' is positively charming in comparison with another old name for London – **the Great Wen**, which conjures up an image of the city as a cyst and its inhabitants as a teeming mass of pus. How much nicer to live in the fruit-growing county of Kent, otherwise known as **the Garden of England**.

Some nicknames come from the physical appearance of a place. Aberdeen is known as **the Granite City** because of the stone used for most of its major buildings, while Kirkcaldy in Fife is **the Long Town** in reference to its mile-long main street. The financial district of London is often referred to as **the Square Mile**, which is a fairly precise description of its size. A more imaginative nickname is **the Venice of the North**, a title bestowed on Birmingham in the nineteenth century on account of it having 174 miles of canals (although the locals are more likely to refer to the city as **Brum**, a shortened form of 'Brummagem', which is itself a variation on the city's old name of 'Bromecham').

Not all places are as precise about the source of their charms. Dumfries is known as **the Queen of the South**, which presumably just means that someone thought it was nicer than the other places in southern Scotland, while Nottingham similarly claims to be **the Queen of the Midlands**.

Other names remain shrouded in mystery. Portsmouth has been known as **Pompey** for as long as anyone can remember, but nobody is exactly sure why this should be. One theory is that ships entering the city's harbour abbreviated the destination Portsmouth Point to 'Pom. P.'.

One of the more recently acquired monikers belongs to Manchester, whose '24-hour party' culture based around the Hacienda nightclub in the early 1990s caused the city to be dubbed **Madchester** – a nickname that is more associated with a particular period of the city's history than the city itself.

Away from all of the mayhem, we arrive in Oxford, home of the country's oldest university. In the nineteenth century the poet Matthew Arnold christened it **the City of Dreaming Spires** in reference to the city's fine architecture and its air of academic calm. Oxford's slightly newer rival Cambridge has been jokingly referred to in contrast as 'the city of perspiring dreams', although in recent years its status as a centre of the technology industry has led to the area around the city acquiring the name **Silicon Fen**.

NOT FROM THESE PARTS, ARE YOU?

Many people think of British English as a distinct 'brand' of the language that can be easily told apart from other forms, like American English or Australian English. While this is true to a large extent, it's not as monolithic as all that. There really is no one stereotypical British accent, despite the efforts of, especially, American actors on television and in films to give the impression of speaking in one! You can break British English down into lots of different **dialects** which each have their own characteristic features, including distinctive local accents, and vocabulary, such as Scottish English, Welsh English and those that belong to regions of England such as the Midlands, the south-west, or Greater London.

Dialects should not be thought of as different, albeit quite closely related, languages. People who use dialect terms, grammar, or pronunciation still understand and use standard English, and dialects are on the whole mutually intelligible. It takes a pretty strong regional accent to mask meaning altogether for a stranger! The nationwide popularity of regionally set television soap operas shows how Brits in different parts of the country soon get used to deciphering localized speech, from the 'Leave it out, John' of London's *EastEnders* to the 'Happen I might want summat' of the Manchester-located *Coronation Street*. A Scouser (a person from Liverpool) will essentially have no problem in conducting a meaningful conversation with a Geordie (a person from Tyneside) or a denizen of Essex.

There are various different reasons to explain how dialects evolve. In Britain's case, English developed out of the language of the Anglo-Saxons, and dialect variations have been traced back many centuries. This is why dialects get started, but why do they persist?

One reason is that in the centuries before mass communication became possible, most people didn't travel very far from their birthplace, and strangers who spoke in a markedly different way were few and far between. In this way, regional differences could become established, as all children growing up in a geographically defined, sometimes quite isolated, area would learn to speak in the same way as the surrounding adults. To some extent, the pre-Norman-Conquest division of Old English into Mercian, Northumbrian, Kentish, and West Saxon dialects has left a recognizable mark on the English of today.

The influence of other languages of the British Isles has also played a large part. Much of the country was under the rule of Danes and other Vikings in the Old English period and the Norse languages contributed many words and pronunciations to these particular areas. The Celtic tongues of the British peoples who inhabited these islands before the speakers of English arrived were often displaced but rarely extinguished. They survived above all in Scotland, Wales, and Northern Ireland, and these places still retain distinctive local dialects which include many borrowed words and expressions.

Dialects are nothing if not resilient and they tend to resist being assimilated by a standardized form. Until the latter half of the twentieth century it was assumed in Britain that those who wanted to get ahead in society had to speak the 'posh' variety of English known as **Received Pronunciation** (often shortened to RP), which itself really only began as the dialect of southern Britain. This was even known as 'BBC English' as it was the form favoured by broadcasters. Rapid social change, especially from the 1960s onwards, helped undermine its predominance until nowadays increasingly fewer of us 'speak like the Queen' and the BBC abounds in fairly undiluted regional accents.

MAYBE IT'S BECAUSE
I'M A LONDONER

When we talk about Britain's capital city as having its own dialect, we automatically think of **Cockney** speech. This of course is essentially a working-class dialect. Middle-class and upper-class Londoners will be more likely to 'talk posh', speaking a version of Received Pronunciation. Whether or not we can still speak of such hard-and-fast class divisions in today's socially fluid Britain is debatable, but it can still serve as a useful starting point when looking at how different groups of people actually speak.

Not all working-class Londoners are Cockneys. Traditionally, qualifying as a true Cockney means being born within the sound of **Bow Bells** (the church bells of St Mary-le-Bow) in the city's East End. Apart from its famous rhyming slang, Cockney speech is most noticeably characterized by the failure to pronounce the letter H at the beginnings of words, (although the dropping of aitches also occurs in other English dialects), the pronunciation of a soft 'th' in the middle of words as 'v' ('I'm in bovver with me muvver'), and the substitution of an 'f' sound for a hard 'th' ('She's an afflete').

Another familiar feature is the habit of tagging on a question at the end of a statement, as if seeking approval or confirmation, often from people who can't really be expected to be in a position to agree or disagree ('He only went and lost it, didn't he? I've gone round to his gaff, haven't I? And he's not even in, is he? It's enough to make you sick, innit?'). This 'innit' tag is, of course, a shortened form of 'isn't it' but such is its popularity that it is often hung on to the end of a statement in which 'isn't it' doesn't make any logical sense, as in, 'I'm feeling a bit rough, innit?' It even turns up in **Hinglish**, the dialect of many British Asians, which is a mixture of Hindi and English.

In the later part of the twentieth century, increasing numbers of people who were raised as middle class began to affect a pseudo-Cockney accent, often because they were involved in the creative arts and sounding too well bred would not be good for their street credibility. This type of speech was soon labelled **Mockney** and it quickly caught on throughout the Home Counties and beyond.

Some of the true Cockney language traits spread outside the city to other parts of south-east England, mainly bordering the estuary of the River Thames, giving rise to a dialect identified as **Estuary English**. The popular television reality show *The Only Way is Essex*, based around inhabitants of parts of Essex, helped expose this way of speaking to a national audience. It has been claimed that Estuary English has been adopted by many middle-class people who don't want to appear snobbish but wouldn't feel comfortable in adopting the full Mockney mode. It used to be taken for granted that the Royal Family would always be a bastion of refined English speaking, but nowadays younger Royals will be heard to speak with a distinct **glottal stop** – a linguist's way of labelling the habit of swallowing the letter 't' rather than pronouncing it sharply.

In the twenty-first century, the mix of London's population is more multicultural than ever, and this is reflected in the speech of its young people. The way many of them speak has been called **Jafaikan**, the idea being that people who are not of Afro-Caribbean descent are mimicking the pronunciation and vocabulary of Jamaicans, but the truth is that many more influences than this are involved in this phenomenon, including the English of Asia and West Africa.

HAVE A BUTCHER'S AT THIS!

One of the most enjoyable aspects of Cockney English is its famous **rhyming slang**. The way this works is that a particular word is replaced by a phrase, usually of two words but sometimes more, the last element of which rhymes with the original word. What makes it even more difficult to decipher for the uninitiated is that the rhyming word is often dropped. A well-known example of this is **apples and pears**, meaning 'stairs', which can be shortened amongst those in the know to **apples**, as in 'Time to head up the apples'.

Nobody knows how long this kind of linguistic game has been around, but examples were recorded in London as long ago as the middle of the nineteenth century. The people using it were typically market traders, who incorporated it into their sales patter. One theory is that it was a means of disguising what they were saying, in order to confuse customers who might be having the wool somewhat pulled over their eyes. But then again, maybe it was just for fun. Whatever the reason, one of its effects was to help promote a sense of community, of being an insider, in a similar way to being in on a shared joke.

It's not just everyday words that are used to provide the rhymes. Often, the names of people or places, real or fictional, are brought into play, as in **Ruby Murray**, meaning a 'curry', or **Hampstead Heath**, meaning 'teeth'. This is one of the main indications that rhyming slang is continually being invented, as the names of contemporary people come into use, often replacing names that would have been familiar only to older generations. In this way **Tony Blairs** now stands for 'flares', and **Britney Spears** does duty for 'beers'.

Here's a brief glossary, with the rhyming word shown in brackets if it is often omitted:

adam and eve	believe
Ayrton Senna	tenner, i.e. ten pounds
barnet (fair)	hair of one's head
boat race	face
boracic (lint)	skint, i.e. penniless
brown bread	dead
butcher's (hook)	a look
china (plate)	mate, i.e. a friend
cream-crackered	knackered, i.e. very tired
daisy roots	boots
dog and bone	phone
dustbin lids	kids
frog and toad	road
Hank Marvin	starvin(g), i.e. very hungry
jam jar	car
loaf (of bread)	head
mutt and jeff	deaf
north and south	mouth
pen and ink	stink
Pete Tong	wrong
plates of meat	feet
rabbit (and pork)	talk
rosie (lee)	tea
skin and blister	sister
syrup (of figs)	wig
trouble and strife	wife
weasel and stoat	coat

THERE'S WELSH, BOYO!

What is now Wales was, in medieval times, one of the regions of Celtic Britain in which the English language of the Anglo-Saxon conquerors never completely replaced the native tongue. While the fortunes of Welsh as a living language have undergone periodic declines and revivals it is undeniable that the brand of English spoken in Wales has been markedly influenced by it.

A fair number of words that originated in Welsh have become established in standard English over the centuries. For example, **flannel**, **flummery**, and – surprisingly perhaps – **penguin** (derived from two Welsh words meaning 'head' and 'white'). A **cromlech** is a term in archaeology for a prehistoric circle of standing stones, and this comes from Welsh words meaning 'bent' and 'flat'. Most people know that a **coracle** is a type of small round boat, and where would the Queen be without her beloved **corgis** ('dwarf dogs' in the original Welsh)?

In Welsh English we can immediately identify several words that have come almost undiluted from the indigenous language. The adjective **bach**, meaning little, is highly familiar as an endearment, as in 'How are you, Emlyn bach?' In geographical contexts, the word **cwm**, meaning a valley, is a recognized part of many place names such as Cwmbran, and is also a general term for a steep-sided basin formation in a mountain landscape. The celebrated annual arts festivals of Wales are known exclusively by their Welsh-language name, the **eisteddfod**. The Welsh drinking toast **iechyd da** (literally, 'good health') is well known amongst non-Welsh people – even if outsiders tend to pronounce it (or even spell it!) as 'yakky da'. One thing we don't want to hear is the exclamation of disgust or abhorrence, **ach-y-fi!**

As well as these more widely understood expressions, there are also many other terms that are more strictly confined to Welsh dialects of English (and it should be remembered that there is considerable variation between different areas of Wales). These include:

bosh	a kitchen sink
cleck	gossip
cootch	a hiding or storage place; also to cuddle
jib	a deliberately contorted face
scag	a tear in fabric
shinkin	a worthless person
sket	to splash water
spag	to scratch
spreathed	painful, especially because of chapping
stingy	a stinging nettle
tamp	to bounce
twp	stupid
wus	a term of address

Some of the language characteristics we associate with Welsh English are more to do with how Welsh people use English words or phrases in particular ways. '**Boyo**', a term of address to a male of practically any age, is really only a variation of 'boy'. The word 'there' is often used in a way not found in standard English, as in 'There's lovely!' (Most English speakers would say something more like 'Isn't that lovely!') and 'see' is often tacked on to a statement in emphasis (as in 'It's just not good enough, see.'). One or two other constructions are perhaps less common than they once were, and could nowadays attract the accusation of portraying a kind of 'stage Welsh' found only in drama rather than in the everyday conversation of Welsh people. These include beginning a sentence with 'Look you', as if to gain someone's attention, or inverting the usual order of words in expressions like 'Fed up, I am!'

I'LL BE IN SCOTLAND AFORE YE

Is there such a thing as the Scots language? It all depends on how you look at it, and this in turn often varies according to how you stand on the political question of Scottish independence. Leaving the latter aside, it can be said without doubt that Scots is descended from Old English in much the same way as modern English is. The Anglo-Saxons who settled in what became England would have had few problems in communicating with their cousins who ventured further north in their quest for lands to conquer.

One of the reasons why Scottish English began to diverge from southern English was the influence on it of the Celtic languages of the native peoples. The Scots themselves had actually moved over from Ireland in the sixth century and spoke a form of Gaelic, and for centuries their language was known as **Erse** (or Irish) to non-speakers, who would have described themselves as speaking English.

Here are some of the words of Gaelic origin that are still in common use in the English of Scotland, and even further afield:

ben	a mountain (often in particular names, as in Ben Nevis or Ben Lomond)
cairn	a mound of stones
ceilidh	an evening of Scottish music and dancing
clan	a family
gillie	a hunter's attendant
glen	a valley
loch	a lake (as in Loch Lomond or Loch Ness)
plaid	a length of cloth worn across the body

shindig	a lively event
slogan	a battle cry
trousers	(from *trouse*)
whisky	(from *uisge-beatha*, literally 'water of life')

While everyone will recognize a Scottish accent – saying things like 'nicht' rather than 'night' and sounding the 'wh' in words such as 'whale' or 'what' like 'hw' – it doesn't do to assume that there is only one such accent. Various parts of Scotland have their own distinctive accents and there are some highly localized vocabularies. People from the north-east who speak **Doric** sound very different from natives of the Central Belt or the Gaels of the Highlands and Islands.

Many expressions common in Scottish English are not immediately identifiable as specific to Scotland – not always even to Scots themselves! Take the ordinary English word 'doubt', for example. If a Scot says 'I doubt it'll rain' he or she doesn't mean that they think it won't rain but that they think it will! A Scottish parcel service will 'uplift' an item rather than rather than 'collect' or 'pick it up'. Scots pick blackberries but they call them 'brambles', and to them a sandwich is 'a piece'.

Here's short glossary of terms that are common in Scottish speech and writing:

afore	before
agley	askew or wrong
ashet	a shallow oval dish or large plate
baffies	slippers
barrie	(in Edinburgh or the east) good or attractive

beastie	an insect or small animal
bidie-in	a live-in partner to whom one is not married
birk	a birch tree
birl	to spin
bodach	an old man
brae	a hillside or steep road
braw	fine or excellent
breeks	trousers
bubbly jock	a turkey
burn	a stream
buttery	(in the north-east) a butter-rich bread roll
byke	a wasps' nest
cantrip	a magic spell or mischievous trick
carnaptious	bad-tempered
clachan	a small village
clappy-doo	a type of large black mussel
clishmaclaver	idle talk or gossip
clootie dumpling	a rich fruitcake boiled in a cloth
corbie	a crow
crowdie	a type of soft white cheese
daud	a lump or chunk
doo	a pigeon or dove
dreich	dreary
eejit	an idiot
fankle	a tangle or to tangle something

feart	frightened
finnan haddie	a smoked haddock
footer	to potter about or fiddle with something
gang	to go
gey	very
girn	to complain or moan
glaikit	foolish
greet	to weep
grue	to shudder, especially through fear or disgust
guddle	a mess or state of untidiness
hauf	a half
hirple	to limp
Hogmanay	New Year's Eve
hurl	a lift or journey in a car
jag	an injection
jaggy	prickly
jenny longlegs	a crane-fly
kenspeckle	well known
laird	a lord or landowner
law	a hill
loon	(in the north-east) a boy or lad
lum	a chimney
machair	sandy, grassy land just above the water line at a sea shore
mowdie	a mole (the burrowing animal)

muir	a stretch of moorland
nane	none
ned	a young male hooligan
numpty	a stupid person
oose	dust or fluff
partan	a crab
peedie	(in Orkney and Caithness) small
peerie heels	stiletto heels
pinkie	the little finger
puddock	a frog or toad
quaich	a small shallow drinking cup
queenie	a shellfish, a type of scallop
quine	(in the north-east) a girl or young woman
radge	(in Edinburgh and the east) very angry
rammy	a noisy disturbance or quarrel
rumbledethump	a dish of cabbage and mashed potato
scunner	to irritate or disgust
sheugh	a gutter or ditch
shilpit	thin and weak-looking
shoogle	to rock, shake, or sway
skelf	a splinter of wood (such as gets stuck in one's finger)
skirlie	a dish of oatmeal and onions fried together
smirr	drizzly rain
smout	a small person

spaewife	a woman who can supposedly tell fortunes
stank	a drain or gutter
stour	dust
stramash	an uproar or brawl
stravaig	to wander
swither	to hesitate or be unable to make up one's mind
syne	since
tait	a small amount or piece of something
tapsalteerie	upside down
tattie-bogle	a scarecrow
teuchter	a Lowlander's term for a Highlander
thrang	busy
thrapple	the throat or windpipe
tumshie	a turnip
vennel	a lane
voe	(in Orkney and Shetland) a bay
wabbit	tired
wean	(in the west) a child
Weedgie	(in Edinburgh) a Glaswegian
wheen	a large number
wheesht!	be quiet!
wynd	a narrow street or lane
yin	one

IN SUNSHINE
OR IN SHADOW

The north-eastern corner of Ireland is a beautiful part of these islands with a troubled past but a more hopeful future. Here we will take a brief look at its language through some of the events that have shaped its history.

The Normans who invaded England eventually turned their attentions to Ireland where **Irish Gaelic** was spoken. This era was known as the **Lordship of Ireland**, but eventually the Gaels regained control over most of the island – apart from the fortified area around Dublin, known as the Pale. The invaders had little authority elsewhere '**beyond the Pale**'.

The language of the north of the island was Gaelic until the seventeenth century. Then large numbers of settlers from Anglican England and Protestant Scotland arrived in a large-scale colonization organized by the Crown that has become known as the **Plantation of Ulster**. The Scottish settlers brought with them their form of Lowland Scots language known as **Lallans**. It eventually became the dominant form of English spoken in Ulster and became known as **Ulster-Scots** or **Ullans** (a blend of *Ulster* and *Lallans*). The Scottish connection means that the north of Ireland is sometimes known as the **Wee North** due to the frequency with which the Scots word 'wee' (meaning small) is used there. Derry (also called Londonderry) is also known informally as the **Wee City** for the same reasons.

The descendants of the original Gaelic-speaking Irish inhabitants share Northern Ireland with those who are descended from the settlers, and this means that the English spoken here also has some Gaelic vocabulary.

Here is a brief glossary of words spoken in Northern Ireland. Words from Irish Gaelic are identified as such.

affrontit	embarrassed
agin	against
aiblins	possibly
auldrife	ancient
banshee	a female supernatural spirit (*Gaelic*)
beetlyheids	tadpoles
bein	cosy
big	to build
boxty	a potato pancake (*Gaelic*)
brae	a hill
bruckle	fragile
caranaptious	bad-tempered
clabber	mud (*Gaelic*)
cleek	a hook
clock	a beetle
coup	to tip over
crack	humorous talk
creesh	grease
cruddle yer sook	to upset yourself
cutty	a girl
danner	a stroll
dicht	to wipe
dingen	very good (*Gaelic*)
disjaskit	neglected
drookit	drenched
duncher	a cap
eariwig	an earwig

eejit	a foolish person
fash	to worry
feart	afraid
fecht	to fight
ferly	a marvellous thing
ferntickles	freckles
flooster	to flatter
forfoughten	exhausted
forrit	forward
galore	in abundance *(Gaelic)*
glaikit	daft
greet	to cry
gulder	to shout
gulley	a carving knife
gurly	windy
hairst	harvest; Autumn
hame	home
hinmaist	last
hirple	to limp
hurchin	a hedgehog
hurdies	hips
jook	to evade
ken	to know
kist o' whistles	a church organ
kitter	a left-handed or clumsy person *(Gaelic)*
kye	cattle
lowe	a fire

lum	a chimney
mass	respect *(Gaelic)*
meg-mony-feet	a centipede
mony	many
Norn Iron	a nickname of Northern Ireland
omadhaun	a fool *(Gaelic)*
oxter	an armpit
prittaes	potatoes
quare	good; strange
runkles	wrinkles
scunge	to roam
shoogly	rickety
siller	silver; money
skinkle	to glitter
smig	chin *(Gaelic)*
smithereens	shattered fragments *(Gaelic)*
snoot-cloot	handkerchief
soor dook	buttermilk
syne	ago
thole	to endure
thon	that
thrapple	the throat
wabbit	tired
wean	a child
wee	small
wittens	knowledge
yestreen	yesterday

A LIFE ON THE
OPEN ROAD

The **Romany** people can trace their lineage back to the Indian subcontinent and can be found across Europe. There are two main branches of the Romany people in Britain, the Romanichals and the Kale, who live predominantly in Wales. They arrived around the beginning of the fifteenth century, and have been given a rough time ever since.

From the moment of their arrival these people, with their strange language, belief structure, travelling ways and allegiances, were viewed with suspicion by the rulers of Britain. Laws banning their entry were introduced as early as 1530, and there is evidence that in the seventeenth century Oliver Cromwell shipped Romany people to the Americas to be slaves on the plantations, along with Catholic children and any other repressed minority he could find. In the Second World War they, like the Jews, were subjected to mass murder by the Nazis, in what they have called the 'Porajmos', or 'Devouring'.

Today they are still viewed with suspicion by many people, and yet remain as defiant and as visible as ever, with customs that have survived many storms. A highlight of the year is the **Appleby Horse Fair**, which has been held since 1750, and is an amazing spectacle. Here one can see at first hand the mastery they have over horses, hear their wonderful music, and get a glimpse of a culture that is usually hidden from our eyes.

The Romany counting system is a rather wonderful thing, perhaps made even more so in that through it we can see tangible links to their Indian past. The numbers one to five (*yek, duy, trin, shtar, panj*) are very similar to those in Hindi, and the name for the number five is the same word that is found in the name 'Punjab' (which roughly means 'land of five rivers').

The Romany language has made some interesting contributions to English. Here are a few examples:

barrie	very good or attractive (in Scots)
chav	a young working class person, considered offensive to some
chiv or **shiv**	a knife
cosh	a blunt weapon
cove	a fellow or chap
deek	to look at
didicoy	one of a group of travellers who live like gypsies but aren't Romany
gadgie	a fellow
gorgio	a non-gypsy
mush	a term of address
nark	a spy or undercover policeman
pal	a close friend
pong	a smell
posh	smart or elegant
radge	angry or in a rage
Roma	a male gypsy
rum	strange or odd
rye	a gentleman
stir	prison
wonga	money

WESTWARD HO!

The south-west region of England is popularly known as **the West Country** and is made up of the counties of Cornwall, Devon, Somerset, Dorset, and Wiltshire. Most British people who don't come from this area tend to think of the south-west dialect in terms of a stereotypical accent, full of meaningless exclamations like 'oo-arr', addressing people as 'ee', references to farming, saying 'zider' instead of cider (inevitably perceived as the local drink of choice!), and constructions like 'I be'. The acting profession even has a name for this kind of generic 'yokel' accent – **Mummerset**, a blend of 'mummer' (an old word for actor) and Somerset.

In fact, the different counties in this part of England have recognizably different dialects. In Cornwall, for example, the English language was slower to become dominant than in more central regions. Cornish, a Celtic language related to Breton, was commonly spoken until the eighteenth century, and this left its mark on the English of Cornwall. Even today, enthusiasts are trying to revive it as a living language and one of the most visible signs of this are the car-stickers displaying '**Kernow**', the Cornish name for the county.

It is true that the West Country abounds in rich farming land and it is no surprise that the dialect often reflects agricultural concerns. The use of rural dialect is marked in the locally set novels of Thomas Hardy, RD Blackmore, and other English literary classics. However, the region also has ancient ties to the seagoing life – both Sir Francis Drake and Sir Walter Raleigh were West Country men and spoke in strong regional accents – and the clichéd pirate in movies from the various versions of *Treasure Island* to the *Pirates of the Caribbean* series is usually portrayed as speaking in this way. In a more modern connection, Devon and Cornwall are famous for providing some of the best surfing locations in Britain. The port city of Bristol is often described as having its own dialect, labelled 'Bristolian'.

Here's a short glossary of West Country dialect:

angle-twitch	an earthworm
appledrain	a wasp
biller	the stem of a plant
charm	a loud noise
coomb	a short valley
cowflop	a foxglove
dawbake	a stupid person
dew snail	a slug
dimpsy	twilight
drangway	a narrow lane
dumbledore	a bumblebee
emmet	(in Cornwall) an ant; also a tourist
grockle	a tourist
gurt	great (in size)
homescreetch	a mistle thrush
hornywink	a lapwing
janner	a person from Plymouth
macky	big
my lover	a term of address to anyone (not just a paramour!)
quist	a wood pigeon
slight	ill
spuddle	a stupid person
vutty	dirty
want knap	a molehill

BOSTIN' BRUM

When most people who are not from the region think about the English Midlands, they tend to think of **Birmingham** or **the Black Country**. As the second-largest city in the United Kingdom, Birmingham (affectionately known as 'Brum') has long been an industrial city but it can boast two cathedrals and three universities, as its natives (the 'Brummies') would be quick to point out. The Black Country was so named for the dense clouds of smoke and soot that once poured from its blast furnaces and foundries. In these post-industrial times the label has become less apposite, but there is still plenty of manufacturing going on there.

Many have described the Midlands accent as unattractive, but it is really no more off-putting than many pronounced regional English accents, and the area has a strong and vibrant set of dialects, elements of which can be traced right back to Anglo-Saxon times. Perhaps there is an element of snobbery in some people's attitudes to the Midlands accent, arising from the area's former image as the home of nothing but 'dark satanic mills'. Certainly in Victorian times 'Brummagem' the informal name for Birmingham from which 'Brum' is derived, was a byword for cheap and flashy products, such as imitation jewellery.

The area of Staffordshire known as **the Potteries** (because of its long involvement in the china and earthenware industries) is also rich in dialect, and this was memorably exploited in the novels of Arnold Bennett (1867–1931) which are largely set in what were known as the 'Five Towns'.

Midlands dialect is full of unusual and quirky vocabulary. Here is a selection:

airtsy-mairtsy	affected or effeminate
all over the occy	in every direction
bellock	to shout
bibble	a pebble

bobowler	a large moth
borm	to smear something with paint, oil, etc
bostin'	excellent
cagmag	shoddily or incompletely finished; also to chat idly
chellup	noise
chelp	to chatter
coating	a telling-off
cubby	short and plump
gowl	the dried mucus found in one's eye corners after sleeping
gradely	fine or excellent
kerky	stupid
laipse	to beat
mackle	to mend something in a makeshift or hurried way
modge	to do something shoddily
nisgul	the smallest and weakest of a brood of chickens
oaky	an ice cream
quist	a wood pigeon
raker	a large lump of coal
rammle	a hoard of possibly useful items
roarming	severe
scrawp	to scratch itchy skin
screet	to weep
scrorp	a deep scratch
slorm	to wipe carelessly
strayve	to wander
tab-hang	to eavesdrop
tocky	muddy
yampy	a foolish person
yorp	to shout

OF MANCS
AND SCOUSERS

Lancashire, in north-west England, is a county of contrasts, both geographical and linguistic. Most of its inhabitants are happy to call themselves Lancastrians but not the people who live on Merseyside, which is effectively a county within a county.

Lancashire was the heartland of the Industrial Revolution, where railways and ship canals were pioneered and mill owners were so wealthy they were called 'cotton kings'. Such hard-headed men were not in favour of state intervention and the **Manchester school** of economists espoused free-market principles. This city grew hugely in the nineteenth century and the leading role it played in Britain's economy was expressed in the phrase 'what Manchester says today, the rest of England says tomorrow'.

The county has lost most of its old industries and some of its towns have been depopulated. Manchester, though, has reinvented itself of late. Its streets have become gentrified and in the last thirty-five years it has spawned many of Britain's favourite musical acts. Football is also big business and the two Manchester clubs are among the world's richest.

Speech in Lancashire is similar to that of other northern counties, although Lancastrians tend to sound the letter 'r' in a pronounced way in words such as 'start' and 'board'. They also lengthen vowels in words such as 'book' and 'look'. The Lancashire accent is a familiar one. Britain's longest-running soap, *Coronation Street*, is set in a fictional suburb of Manchester called Weatherfield where characters refer to one another by the affectionate term 'chuck', and express surprise by exclaiming 'Ee!', or say that something is worthless by calling it 'bobbins'.

The food in Lancashire is hearty and **bagging** (afternoon tea) might consist of a **barm cake** and cheese. This and other Lancashire delicacies such as **hotpot** and **black pudding** are explained elsewhere in this book.

Food also plays a role in the name of Lancashire's other tribe. These are the inhabitants of Liverpool and Merseyside who are known as **Scousers**. Their dialect is **Scouse** and comes from the Germanic word *lobscouse*, which was a sailor's stew of meat, vegetables, and anything else to hand in the galley. Liverpool, until fairly recently, was a major port and many nationalities would have mingled on Merseyside in its glory days. The city is home to one of the oldest Chinese communities in Europe but it is perhaps best known for its Irish heritage. The Irish connection partly explains the accent, although traders and sailors from Scotland, Wales, Scandinavia, Holland, and Germany would have added to the mix.

Scouse dialect has many words not found elsewhere in England, and not even elsewhere in Lancashire. The word **Liverpudlian** itself reveals the playfulness of the Scouse character as 'puddle' is jokingly substituted for 'pool'. Affectionate terms abound on Merseyside. **La**, **wack**, and **wacker** are words for 'pal', **queen** is used to a woman, and **kidder** to anyone. A **scally** (short for 'scallywag') is a rogue whose behaviour is anything from the boisterous to the criminal which might lead him to encounter the **bizzies** or **scuffers** (police officers).

If a Scouser tells you to **do one** he wants you to get lost, and he might refer dismissively to someone from more rural parts of Lancashire as a **woollyback**. Rivalry with the **Mancs** (inhabitants of Manchester) is keen, whether in business, music, or, particularly, football where the Reds of both cities (Liverpool FC and Manchester United) have a particularly fierce rivalry.

Finally, Scousers have a habit of shortening words and then adding 'y or 'ie'. So electricity becomes 'leccy', Christmas becomes 'Chrizzie', and one's best pal, la, or wacker is your 'bezzie mate'.

A YORKSHIRE
COMPLIMENT

Many Englishmen describe their home patch as 'God's own country' but in one county they really mean it. Put on your flat cap and join us as we head up north for a celebration of the history, culture, and language of Yorkshire.

The ancient Romans made York the centre of government for North Britain and called it Eboracum. Two Emperors died here and one, Constantine the Great, was born in the city. When the Romans departed the city became Eoforwic, and when the Vikings invaded in the ninth century they renamed it Jórvík, from which the modern names of York and Yorkshire are derived.

During the fifteenth century civil wars raged in England, with one side represented by a red rose, the other by a white one. This was not a struggle between the counties of Yorkshire and Lancashire – as some might think nowadays – but one between two competing Royal dynasties: the House of Lancaster (the red rose) and the House of York (the white). The two Houses eventually united under the Tudor monarchs, as did the two roses. The roses were later adopted as symbols by the two counties so nowadays cricket matches between Yorkshire and Lancashire are called **Roses Matches**.

Yorkshire is synonymous with cricket, and England's County Championship has been won by Yorkshire a record number of times. Until recently only people born in Yorkshire could play for the club, resulting in many women who happened to be away from the county when heavily pregnant being driven by their cricket-mad husbands to the nearest Yorkshire hospital. The county is also home to the sport of rugby league, where it was born in 1895, and association football's first club side, Sheffield FC, was formed in the county in 1857.

A less well-travelled Yorkshire 'sport' is **ferret legging** where live ferrets are placed down a man's trousers and kept there until he can withstand the pain of the inevitable bites no more. It probably comes from a time when only the wealthy were allowed to own animals for hunting, resulting in poachers hiding ferrets down their trousers.

Perhaps this trial of endurance (for both man and ferret) gave rise to the old expression 'Yorkshire born and Yorkshire bred, strong in the arm and weak in the head'. This is an unusual adage in that most expressions relating to Yorkshire concern the supposed cunning or tight-fistedness of its inhabitants. A **Yorkshire compliment** is a useless gift that costs the donor nothing, a **Yorkshire bite** is a sharp overreaching action, and a **pair of Yorkshire sleeves in a goldsmith's shop** is something worthless. A person who dupes someone might be said to have 'put the Yorkshire' on his victim, and people from other English counties might describe a Scotsman as 'a Yorkshireman with all the generosity squeezed out' – a handy denigration of both Scots and Yorkshire folk.

A culture of distinctness exists in the county. People are more likely to describe themselves as from Yorkshire than from England, the county has its own unofficial anthem 'On Ilkla Moor Baht 'at' (on Ilkley Moor without a hat), and **Yorkshire Day** has been celebrated on August 1st every year since 1975.

The county also has its own dialect. One characteristic is the use of archaic forms such as 'thou' and 'thee' instead of 'you', and 'sen' rather than 'self' (so that 'myself' becomes 'missen'). Another feature is the elimination of unnecessary letters so that 'the' becomes 't'' and 'of' becomes 'o''. The dropping of the letter 'h' is common and is especially noted with the word 'happen' which becomes ''appen' and, when used at the start of a sentence, means 'maybe'.

Here's a selection of words that crop up in Yorkshire dialect:

alicker	vinegar
'appen	maybe, possibly
attercop	a spider; a peevish person
aumery	a cupboard or pantry
backendish	autumnal
badly	ill, poorly
baht	without
bap	a bread bun
barm	yeast
barrow	a person's rightful concern or interest
bartled	smothered in something unpleasant
beck	a stream or brook
belder	to bellow
belm	money
bent	heath or moorland
biggerstang	a builder's scaffolding pole
blake	(of skin complexion) sallow
bleck	thick, fatty, and dirty oil
blut	an elderly lady
bocken	to retch or vomit
bockle	a bottle
boggart	a ghost
brass	money
braunch	to boast
bray	to beat
brew	a hill

brig	a bridge
broddle	to poke around in
cat ice	frozen pools of water
champion	excellent; first rate
cheb	to throw
chelp	to answer back
chuddy	chewing gum
chunter	to mutter or mumble
clough	a ravine
cludger	a toilet
cock loft	an attic
collop	a thick slice
cop	to catch hold of
crake	a crow
creel	a frame for drying clothes
croggy	a ride on the crossbar of a bicycle
dawly	sad or depressed
dimp	a cigarette butt
dolly-posh	left-handed
dowly	dismal and dull
dree	lonely, weary
ee by gum!	Good lord!
ettle	to attempt
fettle	to mend or tidy
fond	foolish
frosk	a frog
fuddle	an informal meal; a buffet

gegs	glasses
gie ower	to stop
ginnel	an alleyway
gloppened	amazed, astounded
goff	to smell bad
goosegog	a gooseberry
grand	excellent; first rate
hagg	a wooded area
jonnock	genuine
laik	to play; to skive
lenerky	soft or floppy
loppy	flea-ridden
lownd	a gentle spring rain
mardy	moody or irritable
mash	(of tea) to brew
Mester	Mister
mither	to bother
neb	the front of a flat cap
nithered	feeling very cold
nobbut	only
now then	hello
nowt	nothing
ower	over
owt	anything
paggered	very tired
pike	a glance
pikelet	a crumpet
powfagged	fatigued, exhausted

radged	very angry
rammel	rubbish
reek	smoke
reyt	right
riding	any of the three administrative areas of Yorkshire
rop	a paunch
sackless	useless
scran	food
seg	a metal stud in the shoe
sen	the self; the inner being
shack	to shake
sithi, sithee	look here!
skerrick	a small amount
skrike	to cry
slart	to rain
Spanish	liquorice
spelk	a splinter
spice	sweets
spuggy	a sparrow
summat	something
tatahash	a cheap stew
thissen	yourself
while	until
winter hedge	a clothes horse
wuthering	blowing strongly with a roaring wind
yam	home
yitten	frightened

HOWAY, MAN!

The north-east of England is one of the most distinctive and proud areas of Britain. People who come from the rest of the United Kingdom may consider everyone who lives between the River Tees and the Scottish border to be **Geordies**, but to people within the North-East that word has a narrower meaning and refers exclusively to the people of Tyneside: specifically the people of Newcastle on the north bank of the Tyne and Gateshead on the south bank. A native of Newcastle would be apt to refer to the people of nearby Wearside (Sunderland and Durham) as **Mackems** (after the Wearsiders' saying that 'we mak 'em and they tak 'em' – alluding to the fact that ships were traditionally built on Wearside, while the fishing and sailing industries were mainly centred around Tyneside). Inhabitants of the more distant Teesside (the area around Middlesbrough, Hartlepool, and Stockton-on-Tees) are known as **Smoggies** (a name that reflects the pollution associated with the local chemical industry).

Although a true Geordie may only come from the area around Newcastle and Gateshead, all of the dialects spoken in north-east England have much in common. Many words used in this area are simply Standard English words that have altered vowel sounds: 'talk' and 'walk' become 'taak' and 'waak'; 'make' and 'take' become 'mak' and 'tak' or 'mek' and 'tek'; 'cow' and 'now' become 'coo' and 'noo'; 'dead' and 'head' become 'deed' and 'heed'; and 'down' and 'town' become 'doon' and 'toon'. The letter 'v' makes a surprising appearance in Geordie dialect as 'to' becomes 'tiv' and 'do' becomes 'div', while another common transformation involves the letter 'y' popping up after an initial consonant, so that 'boot' becomes 'byeut' and 'cook' becomes 'cyeuk'.

Another characteristic of Geordie is the use of 'yous' a plural form of 'you', and 'wor' to mean 'our'. The latter is often used before a name as a sign of affection, as in 'wor Jackie', the nickname of Newcastle football legend Jackie Milburn.

Many of the dialect words of the North-East are common to other northern versions of English. You might equally hear the words 'aye' (yes), 'badly' (ill), and 'nowt' (nothing) from a native of Yorkshire, while words such as 'baary' (fine), 'bairn' (a child), and 'hoaching' (very full) are also used by Scots.

The conventional industries of coalmining, shipbuilding, and fishing have left their mark on the language and culture of this region. At one time, workers in the regions coal mines developed their own specialized jargon, which was known as **Pitmatic**, but the decline of the coal industry has meant that this has become obsolete. Another influence on the local dialect is the region's proximity to Scandinavia, which meant that it was more strongly affected by the Viking invasions than other parts of Britain.

In the twenty-first century, the North-East is known especially as a centre for culture, with Gateshead boasting the Baltic Centre for Contemporary Art and some striking public art such as the monumental 'Angel of the North'. Meanwhile its lively night-life makes Newcastle a mecca for stag and hen parties.

The language of the region has become more aligned with that of the rest of England, and the accent is regarded as friendly, which has made the area popular as the location of customer-service call centres. Nevertheless, it still contains plenty of words that might not be obvious to someone from outside the North-East, and an explanation of some of these can be found on the following pages.

aad	old
aal	all
aalreet	all right
afore	before
agyen	again
aheyt	in the air
ahint	behind
ayont	beyond
baary	lovely
babby	a baby
baccy chow	chewing tobacco
badly	sick; ill
baggie	a small fish
bagie	a turnip
bairn	a child
bait	food
batchy	extremely angry
blackclock	a cockroach
bleb	a blister
bogey	a cart
boily	soup
bonny	very attractive
bowdy-kite	a pot belly
bowk	to vomit
broon	Newcastle Brown Ale
bullet	a small sweet
bummlor	a bumblebee
caa canny	to take care
canny	very good

chare	a narrow alleyway
chollers	jowls
claggy	sticky
clemmy	a stone
cloot	a cloth
cogley	unsteady
cracket	a stool
cree	a shed
cuddy	a donkey or pony
cyeuk	to cook
daffy	to dress smartly
dancers	stairs
dee	to do
deed	dead
deek	to look at
dene	a valley
divvent	don't
dog	Newcastle Brown Ale
dolly-posh	left-handed
doon	down
ducket	a pigeonhole or dovecot
dyke	a ditch
elvis	always
fell	a hill
foisty	damp
fower	four
fratchy	irritable
gallowa	a pony
gan	to go

garth	a garden
gowk	a fool
gowpen	a handful
gripe	a garden fork
grozer	a gooseberry
guffie	a pig
hacky	dirty
hadaway!	go away!
heid	a head
hinny	honey
hoppings	a fair
howay!	let's go!
howk	to dig up
hoy	to throw
hyem	home
keek	to peep
kidda	a term of endearment
kyek	a cake
lace	to thrash
leazes	pasture
lonnen	a wooded lane
lowp	to jump
Mackem	a person from Wearside
mafted	excessively hot
mak	to make
marra	a friend
mint	excellent
Monkeyhanger	a person from Hartlepool
mozzy	a mosquito

neet	night
noo	now
palatick	extremely drunk
panhaggerty	a dish made of leftover meat and potatoes
pet	a casual term of endearment
poke	a wallet
reet	right
sackless	useless
scran	food
shan	bad
shuggy-boat	a fairground swing
skelp	to beat
sneck	a door latch
spelk	a splinter
spuggy	a sparrow
stottie cake	a round bread loaf
stowed out	very full
taak	talk
tab	a cigarette
tak	to take
tappy-lappy	headlong
tiv	to
toon	a town
tussy-pegs	teeth
tyek	to take
varry	very
waak	to walk
why aye!	of course!
wor	our
worky-ticket	a layabout

INDEX

Numbers
70 shilling 97
80 shilling 97

A
Aberdeen Angus 104
Abernethy biscuit 90
academy school 21
Act of Supremacy 12
acts of union 10
Advanced Highers 21
advertising 164
advocate 10
aegrotat 18
Aintree 62
A-levels 21
Alfred the Great 30
allotment 48
amateur dramatics 49
analytical engine 126
Angel of the North 37
Anglo-Saxon 134
apple 111
Appleby Horse Fair 206
Archbishop of Canterbury 12
Archbishop of York 12
argy-bargy 73
Ashes 68
association football 64

B
back-to-back 29
badminton 61
bailout 125
Bakewell tart 86
ballroom dancing 53
Banbury cake 86
Bank of England 124
Bank of Scotland 124
bannock 80
bara brith 81
bar billiards 55
barley wine 97
barmbrack 80
barm cake 80
baron 7
baroness 7
barony 7
barrister 10
bashit neeps 79
Bath bun 81
Bath Oliver 90
bearskin hat 15
beating the bounds 51
Beaufort Scale 114
Beavers 23
Becher's Brook 62
Beefeater 14
Beer 184
beer and sandwiches 129
Belisha beacon 27
Bessy Brantail 109

Bible 136
Big Bang 125
Big Ben 8
Big Mavis 109
Big Smoke 38, 186
bird-watcher 108
Birtspeak 123
bitter 97
blackball 22
Black Country 186, 210
Black Monday 125
black pudding 79
Black Wednesday 125
Bleeding Yew 111
blended whisky 99
blue 19
boarding school 20
Boat Race 19
bob 16
Bodyline 69
bog jumper 109
bog snorkelling 59
boiled sweets 88
boil-in-the-bag 95
bolshy 128
book club 23
Boudicca 30
Bow Bells 190
bowler hat 24
boxty 78
Brands Hatch 63
bread 16

bridie 82
Britannia 40
British Bulldog 58
British disease 129
Britishness 40
brown ale 97
Brownies 23
Brum 187
bubble-and-squeak 78
building society 124
Burns Night 98
Burns Supper 79
buttery 80
buzzword bingo 123

C
cabinet 9
Caerphilly 93
called to the bar 10
campus university 18
Carroll, Lewis 142
catchphrase 160
Catherine Tate Show, The 162
ceilidh 52
chambers 10
champ 78
Chancellor of the Exchequer 9
Charlie Muftie 109
Cheddar 92
cheese rolling 59
Chelsea bun 81
Chelsea pensioner 15

Chelsea tractor 27
Chequers 9
chicken tikka massala 95
chip butty 80
chocolate 88
Christmas pudding 84
chucking out time 55
Churchill, Sir Winston 33
Church of England 12
Church of Scotland 13
City, the 39
City of Dreaming Spires 187
city slicker 34
clockwatching 121
Clockwork Orange 26
clootie dumpling 85
closed shop 129
clotted cream 79
Clydesdale 105
Cockney 190
colcannon 78
Colemanballs 72
Colossus 126
Common Riding 51
Commonwealth of Nations 5
commuter belt 121
conkers 58
constitutional monarchy 4, 8
Cook, Peter 158
Cornish cream tea 79
Cornish pasty 82
Coronation chicken 95

cottage loaf 80
cottage pie 83
countess 7
country bumpkin 35
country dancing 52
country estate 29
Countryside Alliance 107
courtroom artist 11
Cowes 62
craft beer 96
cratur 99
cream tea 79
credit crunch 125
cricket 61
croft 28
Cromwell, Oliver 32
crossbencher 8
Cross Keys 57
cross the floor 8
crown 16
crown court 10
Crown Jewels 14
Cubs 23
cuckoo 108
Cuckoo Bush 57
Cumberland sausage 78
curate 12
curry 95

D

Dad's Army 162
daffodil 113
daisy 112
dance hall 52
darts 55
Defender of the Faith 12
deregulation 125
Desmond 19
detached house 29
Devonshire tea 79
dialect 188
diamond jubilee 4
Diana, Princess of Wales 33
Dickens, Charles 143
difference engine 126
division bell 9
doonies 59
Doric 197
Double Gloucester 93
Douglas Hurd 19
downies 59
Downing Street 9
Drake, Sir Francis 32
dram 98
dreich 115
duchess 6
duchy 6
duke 6
Dundee cake 86

E

earl 7
earldom 7
early bath 73
early doors 72
Eccles cake 86
Edinburgh Tattoo 14
eightsome reel 52
eisteddfod 194
elder 13
Elizabeth I 32
emoticon 170
equerry 5
Erse 196
Essex girl 34
Essex man 34
Estuary English 191
Eton Fives 58
Eton wall game 58
euphemism 122, 156
export 97

F

fagging 20
fanzine 65
farls 78, 80
farthing 16
Fast Show, The 162
ferret legging 214
field 106
fiver 16
flexible working 121

florin 16
flying picket 129
football 60
football chants 67
football clichés 66, 72
football phone-in 65
football pools 64
footer 59
Forth Bridge 36
fox-hunting 106
Freemason 22
friendly society 124

G
Garden of England 186
garibaldi 91
gastropub 54
Gay Gordons 52
gazump 28
gazunder 28
GCSE 21
General Assembly 13
General Strike 128
Generation Game, The 163
gentleman's gentleman 35
gentleman's third 18
Gentlemen 68
Gentlemen's club 22
Geoff Hurst 19
Geordie 220
giant vegetables 48
Giggleswick 185

ginger nut 91
Glamorgan sausage 78
glottal stop 191
Gloucester Old Spot 105
gnomes of Zurich 124
golf 61
Goon Show, The 161
government 8
grammar school 21
Grand National 62
Granite City 186
Great Fire of London 38
Great Snoring 184
Great Wen 186
Green Man 57
green-welly brigade 107
Guernsey 104
guest ale 54
Guides 23
guild 120
guinea 16
Gurkah 14

H
haar 115
Hadrian's Wall 37
haggis 79
half-crown 16
ha'penny 16
Harris tweed 25
hauf and a hauf 99
head of state 4

heart of oak 110
heavy 97
heir apparent 5
Henley 62
Henry V 31
hereditary peer 6
Hereward the Wake 30
Highland cattle 104
Highland dress 24
Highland whisky 99
hill lamb 78
Hill O Many Stanes 185
Hinglish 167, 190
hip-hop 166
Hogmanay 98
hoick 106
hopping 50
hot cross bun 81
house 20
House of Commons 8
House of Lords 8
humour 158
hurling the silver ball 59

I
idiom 152
India Pale Ale 97
industrial relations 128
inner-city estate 29
Inns of Court 10
inselaffen 42
interweb 127

Irish Gaelic 202
Island whisky 99
Islay whisky 99
ITMA 161

J
Jafaikan 167, 191
Jam roly-poly 85
jargon filter 123
jellied eels 79
Jelly Babies 89
Jersey 104
jiggery-pokery 73
jobsworth 121
John Bull 40
Johnson, Samuel 158

K
kedgeree 95
Kernow 208
kilt 24
King Arthur 30
King James Version 136
knowledge, the 39

L
Ladies' Day 62
lady-in-waiting 5
Lady of Paliament 7
Lallans 202
Lamb and Flag 57
Lambeth Walk 53

Lancashire hotpot 79
lardy cake 87
laver bread 78
lawyer 10
League Against Cruel Sports
  107
lecture 19
leek 78
Lent term 20
lime 111
limey 42
links 61
liquorice allsorts 89
Little Britain 162
Little Snoring 184
Llanfairpwllgwyngyllgogery-
chwyrndrobwllllantysiliogogogoch
185
lodge 23
lolly 16
London 38
London particular 115
London pride 113
Long Town, the 186
Lord Chief Justice 11
Lord of Parliament 7
Lord's 68
Lordship of Ireland 202
Lords Spiritual 13
Lorne sausage 78
Lost 184
love-lies-bleeding 113

Lowland whisky 99
L-plates 27
Luddite 120

M
macaroni cheese 95
Mackem 220
Madchester 187
Major Oak 110
male-voice choir 35
management-speak 122
Manc 213
Manchester school 212
manse 28
marchioness 6
marquess 6
marquessate 6
martin 108
master of foxhounds 106
Maundy Money 17
MCC 68
member of parliament 8
mess 15
Meteorological Office 114
Metro 26
Metroland 121
Michaelmas term 20
mild 97
military vocabulary 148
millennium bug 127
Milligan, Spike 158
minister 9

Mint 17
mizzle 115
Mizzly Dick 109
mob football 59
Mockney 191
Moderator 12, 13
Molly Washdish 109
monarchy 4
Mondeo man 34
monkey 16
Monty Python's Flying Circus
 159, 162
mop fair 50
Morris Dance 52
music hall 49

N
NAAFI 15
narrowboat 26
nautical vocabulary 146
Nelson, Viscount Horatio 32
New Forest 110
Newton, Sir Isaac 32
new words 176
NICE decade 125
nightingale 109
Nightingale, Florence 33
nobility 6
not cricket 68
not proven 10

O
oak 110
oatcake 90
obsolete words 172
Offa's Dyke 37
Olde Trip to Jerusalem 57
old-fashioned words 172
one-day cricket 69
Only Fools and Horses 163
opposition 9
Orwell, George 143
Owain Glyndŵr 31
Oxbridge 18
Oxford brogues 24

P
pale ale 96
pantomime 49
parish priest 12
Parliament Oak 110
pea-souper 115
Peepy Lennart 109
Pegasus crossing 27
pelican crossing 27
penny farthing 16
pick-and-mix 89
pie and mash 79
pigeon fancying 48
Pitmatic 221
Pity Me 185
pizza 95
plaid 25

Plain English Campaign 123
Plantation of Ulster 202
plate-glass university 18
Players 68
play with a straight bat 68
ploughman's lunch 83, 92
Plum duff 84
Poets' Corner 36
polo 61
Pommy's shower 43
Pompey 187
Pontefract cake 89
pony 16
pork pie 83
porter 96
potato and parsley soup 78
potato scone 78, 80
Potteries, the 186, 210
pound 16
prawn-sandwich brigade 65
Presbyterian 13
primate 12
prime minister 8
private school 20
property ladder 28
proverb 150
pub 54
pub crawl 54
public bar 54
public school 20
pub triathlon 55

Q
Queen of the Midlands 187
Queen of the South 187
Queen's Counsel 11

R
Rainbows 23
Ravenmaster 14
real ale 97
Received Pronunciation 189
redbrick university 18
Red Clydeside 128
redcoat 15
Red Lion 56
rhyming slang 192
rice pudding 85
Richard the Lionheart 31
Riding of the Marches 51
Robert the Bruce 31
robin 108
Robin Hood 31
Romany 206
Ronglish 72
rooinek 42
rosbif 42
rose 113
Rose and Crown 56
Roses Match 214
Routemaster 26
rowie 80
Royal Ascot 62
Royal borough 39

Royal British Legion 23
royal family 4
Royal Oak 57, 110
royal prerogative 4
Royal Society 23
rugby 60
Russell Group 18
rusticate 19

S
sab 107
Sally Lunn 86
saloon bar 54
Saracen's Head 57
Scotch mist 115
Scotch pie 82
Scots law 10
Scott, Captain 33
Scouse 213
Scouser 213
Scout Association 23
Scratchy Bottom 184
sea fret 115
secretary of state 9
semi 29
sent down 19
serf 120
Shakespeare, William 138
Shaw, George Bernard 158
shepherd's pie 83
shepherd's sundial 113
shepherd's weatherglass 113

Sherwood Forest 110
Shetland pony 105
shilling 16
shilly-shally 73
Shipping Forecast 114
ship's biscuit 90
shire horse 105
shop steward 129
shortbread 91
shove ha'penny 55
shrapnel 16
Silicon Fen 187
Silverstone 63
simnel cake 87
Single Gloucester 93
single malt 99
sit-ye-down 109
sixpence 16
sixth form 21
skylark 109
slang 166
Sloane Ranger 35, 167
smiley 170
smirr 115
smog 115
Smoggie 220
snooker 61
snug 54
SOBER decade 125
soda bread 78, 80
solicitor 10
sovereign 16

spaghetti bolognaise 95
Speaker of the Commons 9
Speyside whisky 99
spit and sawdust 54
sporran 25
spotted dick 85
spot the ball 64
Square Mile, the 186
square sausage 78
stagflation 125
St Andrews 63
stargazey pie 82
stately home 29
state school 21
steak and kidney pudding 84
Steel City 186
steeplechasing 60
stenographer 11
Steward of the Chiltern
  Hundreds 8
stiff upper lip 40
Stilton 93
Stinking Bishop 93
Stonehenge 36
stottie cake 80
stout 96
stovies 79
stripping the willow 52
Suffolk Punch 105
Sun, The 159
swearing 168
swing-devil 109
syllabub 85

T
take silk 11
tally-ho 106
Tam o' Shanter 25
Tamworth 105
tanner 16
tap dressing 51
tatties 79
tea break 121
teacake 87
teisen dorth 81
tenner 16
tennis 61
terraced house 29
territorial soldier 14
test match 68
Test Match Special 69
thornproof 25
three-day week 129
three-line whip 9
thruppence 16
tied house 54
tipsy cake 87
toad-in-the-hole 83
toad snatcher 109
Tolpuddle Martyrs 128
Tommy 42
Tommy Atkins 42
Tory 8
tossing the caber 59
toucan crossing 27
Trevor Nunn 19

trews 25
trooping the colour 14
Tube 26
Turk's Head 57
tutorial 19
tweet 171
Twenty20 69
twitcher 108

U
Ullans 202
Ulster Fry 78
Ulster-Scots 202
uniform 20
up-and-under 73
Up-Helly-Aa 51
uppies 59

V
variety 49
varsity match 19
Venice of the North 187
vicarage 28
view halloo 106
viscount 7
viscountcy 7
viscountess 7
voting lobby 9

W
wakes 50
Wallace, Sir William 31
watery pleeps 109
Wee City 202
wee goldie 99
Wee North 202
well dressing 51
Wellington, Duke of 32
Wellington boots 25
Welsh rabbit 78
Welsh rarebit 78, 92
Wensleydale 93
West Country 208
Westminster Abbey 36
Weston-under-Lizard 184
Westward Ho! 185
wheaten bread 80
Whig 8
whingeing Pom 43
whipper-in 106
whisky 98
white-collar worker 121
White Hart 56
White Horse 56
white van man 34
wildcat strike 129
Wilde, Oscar 158
Wimbledon 63
Windsor knot 24
wine gums 88
Winkies 59

Winter of Discontent 129
Woolton pie 83
words of French origin 144
words of German origin 145
words of Italian origin 144
words of Spanish origin 145
Working men's club 22
World Wide Web 127

Y
yaffle 109
yard of ale 54
Yarg 93
yeoman 120
Yeoman Warders of the
  Tower of London 14
Yorkshire Day 215
Yorkshire pudding 84

Z
zebra crossing 27